Adult
English
Three

Adult English Three

John Chapman

Communication Arts Department
LaGuardia Community College

PRENTICE-HALL, INC., Englewood Cliffs, New Jersey 07632

Library of Congress Cataloging in Publication Data
Chapman, John (date)
    Adult English three.

      1. English language—Text books for foreigners.
    I.—Title.
PE1128.C5248   428'.24   77-28336
ISBN   0-13-008862-5

Printed in the United States of America

10   9   8   7   6   5   4   3   2   1

Prentice-Hall International, Inc., *London*
Prentice-Hall of Australia Pty. Limited, *Sydney*
Prentice-Hall of Canada, Ltd., *Toronto*
Prentice-Hall of India Private Limited, *New Delhi*
Prentice-Hall of Japan, Inc., *Tokyo*
Whitehall Books Limited, *Wellington, New Zealand*

ACKNOWLEDGMENTS

To:

Larry Anger, whose imagination helped launch *Adult English*.

Marilyn Brauer, Katharine Glynn, and Irene Springer, who took the time to understand my aims and include me in each step of production.

Friends and colleagues, who contributed countless ideas and put up with a single topic of conversation for so many months.

Many Thanks,

John

Contents

Preface

Adult English is a series of three books for adult students of English as a second language. Pictures, reading passages, and exercises deal with real-world experiences. *Adult English Three* is intended for those who have mastered the basic structures of the English language and have developed a moderate vocabulary. Each unit is carefully planned, requiring the student to take on an increasingly more active and productive role as the lesson progresses. *Adult English Three* offers a review of some basic verb tenses and grammar-related items. It also introduces material suitable for intermediate students.

Photographs have been chosen to illustrate specific grammatical structures and vocabulary words. Photos and drawings form the basis for the introduction and practice of each new language item.

Reading Passages and Questions are used to reinforce the structural focus of the lesson as often as possible. But their main purpose is to develop specific reading skills. *Adult English Three* continues to develop the student's ability to find facts, form inferences, and understand the sequence of events in a story. It also helps students learn how to find main ideas, state main ideas in their own words, and find details to support them. Vocabulary development exercises are included.

Exercises give students intensive language practice in a variety of settings. The exercises guide students in their interaction with the teacher, with another student, and with a small group of students. The subject matter always pertains to adult activities. Students have many opportunities to discuss their own experiences in the context of the exercise.

Structure and *Vocabulary* sections summarize the material presented in each unit. Few grammatical terms are used in the structure section. Vocabulary has been limited (and re-introduced) to allow students to focus on structure items. Blank lines are provided in the vocabulary section so that each class can add its own words—words which enable them to apply the lesson material to their own lives.

Listening Exercises are found at the end of each unit. They are cued to the structure and vocabulary presented. Listening practice serves two purposes: (1) It helps students develop better listening discrimination and (2) it helps the teacher evaluate the listening ability of each class.

The exercises and visual material in *Adult English* lend themselves to a variety of approaches. The teacher's manual suggests some specific ways of presenting each unit. However, teachers will find that a great deal of flexibility is possible. Homework can be used for additional in-class practice. Reading questions can be used for oral practice. Photographs can be used as the basis for writing assignments. The teacher can tailor *Adult English* to fit the interests, needs, and abilities of each individual class.

John Chapman

Adult
English
Three

Unit 1

PICTURE TO TALK ABOUT

Last week these children visited the library for the first time. They heard a story and learned how to take books from the library. The teacher will tell what they did using two-word verbs. Repeat each sentence. Then say the sentences to another student. Later write in the missing words.

Sybil Shelton

PICTURE 1

Name _____ Date _____

Fill-ins

1. The children _____ _____ the teacher.

2. They _____ _____ the pictures in the book.

3. Sometimes they _____ _____ the story.

4. At the end, they _____ _____ it.

5. Later the children _____ _____ another book.

Library Procedures

1. _____ _____ a library card and give it to the librarian.

2. _____ _____ a book.

3. _____ _____ the book before you leave.

4. _____ _____ the book in one week.

5. If you can't return the book in one week, _____ _____

the librarian.

SEPARABLE AND INSEPARABLE TWO-WORD VERBS

Most two-word verbs are separable. That means that you can put a word (or words) between the two parts. Examples A, B, and C are all correct.

Example A: *Fill out* a card.
Example B: *Fill* a card *out*.
Example C: *Fill* it *out*.

*Name*_____ *Date* _____

Other two-word verbs are inseparable. You can't put any words between the two parts. Example D is correct, but Examples E and F are wrong.

Example D: *Listen to* the teacher.

Example E: *Listen* the teacher *to*. (wrong)

Example F: *Listen* her *to*. (wrong)

CHART 1

Separable Two-Word Verbs from this Unit

bring back	fill out
call up	pick out
check out	

CHART 2

Inseparable Two-Word Verbs from this Unit and Adult English Two, Unit 1.

get on	look at
get to	look for
laugh at	talk about
listen to	

ORAL PRACTICE WITH SEPARABLE TWO-WORD VERBS

Say the library procedures three ways. First practice with the teacher, and then with another student. Read the procedure from the book. Then say it again, putting the necessary words between the two parts of the verb. The third time put a pronoun between the two parts.

Example: *Fill out* a library card.

Fill a library card *out*.

Fill it *out*.

QUESTIONS AND ANSWERS

Practice the questions and answers with another student. Use the verbs in Chart 1 and Chart 2. When using separable verbs, put a pronoun between the two parts of the verb in your answer.

Examples: 1. Is the book funny?

Yes, I *laughed at* it.   (inseparable)

Name _____ *Date* _____

2. Did you telephone your sister?

    Yes, I *called* her *up*.   (separable)

3. What are the children doing?

    They are _____ _____ the picture.

4. Do you like music?

    Yes, I _____ _____ _____ all the time.

5. Did you choose that shirt?

    Yes, I _____ _____ _____.

6. Did you finish your registration form?

    Yes, I _____ _____ _____.

7. When will you return that library book?

    I'll _____ _____ _____ next week.

8. Are you trying to find the library?

    Yes, I'm _____ _____ _____.

ORAL PRACTICE

Work in groups of three or four. Chart 3 shows the activities of some school children. Take turns making sentences from the chart using two-word verbs in the past tense, the present continuous tense, and the future tense. When using separable verbs, put the necessary words between the two parts of the verb. (Inseparable verbs are marked with an **X**.)

Name_____ *Date* _____

CHART 3

```
┌─────────────────────────────────────────────────────────────────┐
│   Yesterday Afternoon                    Now                       │
│                                                                    │
│   X get to     — the library      X talk about — their books       │
│                                                                    │
│     fill out   — their cards        check out  — their books       │
│                                                                    │
│   X listen to  — the librarian                                     │
│                                                                    │
│     pick out   — some books                                        │
│                                                                    │
│                        Next Week                                   │
│                                                                    │
│              bring back — their books                              │
│                                                                    │
│            X talk about — their books                              │
│                                                                    │
│            X look for   — more books                               │
│                                                                    │
│              check out  — some more books                          │
└─────────────────────────────────────────────────────────────────┘
```

Examples: They *got to* the library.

They *filled* their cards *out*.

TALK ABOUT THE CHART

Chart 4 shows what Karen did on Monday. The teacher will tell about her day using the sentences below the chart. Repeat each sentence. Then say the sentences to another student. Later write in the missing words.

CHART 4

Time	Event	Time	Event
9:00	got to her office	2:00	went to the dentist
10:00	made some phone calls	3:00	returned home
11:00	wrote letters	4:00	took a nap
noon	went home	5:00	read the newspaper
1:00	had lunch	6:00	had dinner
		7:00	went to a movie

Name _____ *Date* _____

1. Karen made some phone calls _____ she wrote the letters.

2. She stayed at the office _____ noon.

3. She went to the dentist _____ lunch.

4. She went to the dentist at 2:00. _____ she returned home.

5. She returned home at 3:00. _____ she took a nap.

6. She took a nap. _____ she read the newspaper.

7. She took a nap _____ she returned home.

8. She took a nap _____ she read the newspaper.

9. She stayed home _____ 7:00.

10. She had dinner at 6:00. _____ she went out.

CONNECTORS: BEFORE, UNTIL, AFTER, AFTERWARD, AFTER THAT

Work in groups of three or four. After you finish this section, check your answers with the teacher.

7:30 have breakfast
8:00 go to work
5:00 come home

Example 1:   I have breakfast *before* I go to work.

Before I go to work, I have breakfast.

Example 2:   I work *until* 5:00.

Until 5:00 I work.

Example 3:   I have breakfast. *Afterwards* I go to work.

Example 4:   I have breakfast. *After that* I go to work.

Example 5:   I go to work *after* I have breakfast.

After I have breakfast, I go to work.

Circle the numbers in front of the correct completions for each sentence below.

A. Look at Example 1. The words that follow *before* tell about events that happen

   1. earlier than the other half of the sentence.

   2. later than the other half of the sentence.

B. Look at Example 2. The words that follow *until* tell about events that happen

   1. earlier than the other half of the sentence.

   2. later than the other half of the sentence.

C. Look at Example 3. The words that follow *afterwards* tell about events that happen

   1. earlier than the other sentence.

   2. later than the other sentence.

D. Look at Example 4. The words that follow *after that* tell about events that happen

   1. earlier than the other sentence.

   2. later than the other sentence.

E. Look at Example 5. The words that follow *after* tell about events that happen

   1. earlier than the other half of the sentence.

   2. later than the other half of the sentence.

F. Which two connectors are used when you have two separate sentences?

   1. before

   2. until

   3. after

   4. afterwards

   5. after that

Name _____ *Date* _____

TALK ABOUT KAREN

Work in pairs. Take turns using Chart 4 to make sentences about Karen. The first person makes a sentence using *after*. The second person talks about the same two events, but makes two sentences using *afterwards*.

Example: Person 1: Karen made some phone calls after she got to her office.

                Person 2: Karen got to her office at 9:00. *Afterwards* she made some phone calls.

MORE ORAL PRACTICE

Work in pairs again. This time, the first person makes a sentence with *before*. The second person talks about the same two events, but makes a sentence using *after*.

Example: Person 1: Karen took a nap before she read the newspaper.

                Person 2: Karen read the newspaper after she took a nap.

TALK ABOUT YOURSELVES

Work in groups of four or five. First choose one person from the group and make a chart (like Chart 4) using the events in that person's day. Then take turns making sentences using *before*, *after*, and *after that*.

CHART 5

Time	Event	Time	Event

Name _____ Date _____

WRITING PRACTICE

Look at Chart 4. Complete the sentences below using *before*, *after*, and *afterwards* plus any other words you need.

Example: 1. Karen made some phone calls ___before she wrote letters___

2. Karen went home _____ *dentist* _____.

3. She went to the dentist _____ *lunch* _____.

4. She had lunch at 2:00. _____.

5. Karen returned home _____ *newspaper* _____.

6. Karen returned home _____ *dentist* _____.

7. Karen had dinner at 6:00. _____.

8. Karen went to a movie _____ *dinner* _____.

READING PASSAGE

Monday is not my best day, and last Monday was the worst of all. I woke up late, so I tried to hurry. I didn't want to be late to work. First I burned my breakfast, so I couldn't eat it. Then I got coffee on my blouse and I had to change it. While I was washing the dishes, I broke a plate.

I left the house at 8:45. But I forgot my bag, so I had to go home to get it. Of course I was late to work. The boss didn't say anything, but he was looking at me.

At noon I wanted to relax. I went out to buy some new clothes. I was trying on blouses when I looked at my watch. It was 1:00! I would be late to work again. I forgot to take off the store's blouse and put on my own. I dropped my blouse on the table, and started to leave wearing a new blouse. The clerk called, "Hey lady. Aren't you going to pay for that?" My face was really red. Everyone looked at me.

I paid for the blouse. It was 1:15 already. I didn't go back to work. I went right home and got into bed. It was the only safe place for me that day.

Name _____ Date _____

READING QUESTIONS

Fact

Complete the following sentences using the facts in the story on page 9.

1. She hurried because _____.

2. She got coffee on her blouse after _____.

3. Before she broke the plate, _____.

4. She was at home until _____.

5. She worked in the office until _____.

6. She started to leave the store after _____.

7. She paid for the blouse before _____.

8. She went home after _____.

STRUCTURES

Separable Two-Word Verbs

Please	bring		back	your books.
Please	bring	your books	back.	

Inseparable Two-Word Verbs

	Please	look		at	page 32.
(wrong)	Please	look	page 32	at.	

(See Charts 1 and 2 on page 3 for a list of separable and inseparable two-word verbs.)

Name _____ Date _____

I watch television	before	I go to bed.
I watch television	until	11:00.
I go to bed	after	I watch television.

I watch television for an hour.
I watch television for an hour.

Afterwards	I go to bed.
After that	I go to bed.

(See **Connectors**, page 6, for more examples and an explanation.)

VOCABULARY

Nouns	*Verbs*	*Adjectives*	*Other*
activity	hurry	necessary	_____
dentist	pay for	_____	_____
event	return	_____	_____
librarian	take a nap	_____	_____
procedure	_____	_____	_____
story	_____	_____	_____
_____	_____	_____	_____
_____	_____	_____	_____

HOMEWORK

A. During the next class the teacher will write two-word verbs on the blackboard. Be ready to make sentences using each verb. If the verb is separable, you will make two sentences. If it is inseparable, you will make only one sentence.

Name _____ *Date* _____

B. If the sentence is correct, copy it on a separate sheet of paper. If it is wrong, make the necessary changes.

1. Please look me at.

2. I'm looking my brother for.

3. She called me up.

4. Al listened the radio to.

5. At 7:30 we got the bus on.

6. I checked a book out.

C. At home practice *before, after,* and *afterwards* using the events in Chart 5. Be ready to say five or six sentences from your chart during the next class.

D. Make a list of events in your life. (I left my country. I got a job. I got married.) Then write sentences using the connectors from this unit. Try to use each connector at least once.

LISTENING EXERCISE

The teacher will read the following sentences. Fill in the missing words.

1. Al studied for two hours. _____ he took a nap.

2. _____ Al left home, he had lunch.

3. Don't forget to _____ your books.

4. Karen went home _____ she finished work.

5. Did you _____ a new coat?

6. Did you _____ a blue one?

7. _____ they chose books, the children went home.

Name _____ *Date* _____

8. I studied for ten minutes _____ class.

9. Please _____ your books next week.

10. Karen bought a newspaper. _____ she got on the bus.

Unit 2

PICTURE TO TALK ABOUT

Bill is a construction supervisor in California. His boss, Larry, lives in New York. Larry calls Bill every week. Notice the use of *it* in the dialog. Repeat each line after the teacher. Then practice the dialog with another student.

Ford Motor Company

PICTURE 2

Name _____ Date _____

Secretary:	Telephone call, Mr. Long.
Bill:	Who is it?
Secretary:	It's the boss.
Bill:	Hello, Larry. How are you?
Larry:	Fine. How's the weather there? It's snowing here.
Bill:	It's warm and sunny here in California.
Larry:	And how is the job going?
Bill:	No problems. It's fun to work out here. It will take three or four weeks to finish the job. Tomorrow I have to go to Los Angeles for supplies.
Larry:	How far is it?
Bill:	It's about 100 miles. It'll take about five hours coming and going.
Larry:	Well, good luck. It's good to talk with you.
Bill:	Take care of yourself. Good-bye.

ORAL PRACTICE WITH *IT*

Work in pairs. Take turns asking and answering these *it* questions. Use complete sentences. Later write in the missing words.

Example: _____Is it_____ sunny? Yes, _____it's sunny_____ .

1. _____ fun to swim?

   Yes, _____.

2. How far _____ to Miami?

   _____ to Miami.

3. Who _____?

   _____ Karen.

4. How long _____ take?

   _____ two hours.

Name _____ Date _____

15

5. _____ snow in winter?

Yes, _____.

SPECIAL USES OF *IT*

It is a pronoun. *It* often refers to a noun in another sentence.

Example: (My bag) is on the table. Give (it) to me.

In the dialog and exercise above, *it* does not refer to a noun in another sentence. The word *it* fills a space at the beginning of the sentence. In these sentences, *it* is a filler. (*There is* and *There are* are also fillers. See *Adult English Two,* Unit 7.)

In this unit, *it* is used as a filler in five types of sentences.

Type 1—Periods of Time _____

_____

Type 2—Weather _____

_____

Type 3—Distance _____

_____

Type 4—Identification _____

_____

Type 5—It's + adjective + infinitive _____

_____

Review the dialog on page 15. The word *it* appears ten times. Circle the ten *its*. Then copy the ten sentences into the blanks above. You will have two sentences for each type. Ask the teacher to check your answers.

Name_____ Date _____

PARAPHRASING

When you paraphrase a sentence, you tell the same information but you use different words.

Example: Bill is taller than Larry.

Larry is shorter than Bill.

Work in pairs. Paraphrase the following sentences using *it* plus any other necessary words.

1. Who is on the phone? Who ____is it____?

2. I need thirty minutes to walk home. _____ takes

   _____ to walk home.

3. Today is a cold day. _____ today.

4. My house is twenty blocks from here. _____

   to my house.

5. The person who called was Karen. _____ Karen who called.

6. This job will continue for two hours. _____ take

   _____ to finish the job.

7. I enjoy dancing. _____ fun _____.

8. I like to play soccer. _____ fun _____.

9. Yesterday was sunny. _____ yesterday.

10. Alaska is 2,000 miles from here. _____ to Alaska.

GROUP PRACTICE

Take turns asking and answering questions using *it* as a filler. Use the words in the list to make your questions.

How far — to Alaska   Warm — Hawaii

Warm — in Alaska   Cheap — to fly to Hawaii

Expensive — to fly to Alaska   How long — to fly to Hawaii

How long — to fly to Alaska   How far — to Hawaii

WRITING PRACTICE

Write four sets of questions and answers like those in the **Group Practice** section. Write about a country that you have visited or a country that you want to visit.

Question:

  Answer:

Question:

  Answer:

Question:

  Answer:

Question:

  Answer:

PICTURE TO TALK ABOUT

Mr. and Mrs. Miller are farmers. They live in Vermont. The teacher will say ten sentences about them. Repeat each sentence. Then say the sentences to another student. Later write in the missing words.

United Nations

PICTURE 3

1. Past Tense   (buy)   The Millers _____ their farm ten years ago.

2. Present Perfect Continuous Tense   (live)   They _____ _____ _____ there since then.

3. Present Perfect Continuous Tense   (work)   They _____ both _____ _____ seven days a week.

4. Present Continuous Tense   (sit)   Tonight they _____ _____ on the porch.

5. Present Perfect Continuous Tense   (talk)   They _____ _____ _____ about the weather.

6. Present Perfect Continuous Tense   (smoke)   Mr. Miller _____ _____ _____ cigarettes.

7. Past Tense   (invite)   Mrs. Miller _____ the new neighbors to dinner.

Name _____ Date _____

8. Present Perfect   (want)*   She _____ _____ _____ to meet
    Continuous Tense   them for several weeks.

9. Past Tense   (call)   They _____ to say that they would be late.

10. Present Perfect   (wait)   The Millers _____ _____ _____ for half an hour.
     Continuous Tense

Present Perfect Continuous Tense = *have + been + Base form + ing*

See: Present Continuous Tense, *Adult English One,* Unit 2
        Past Tense, *Adult English One,* Units 5 and 6
        Present Perfect Tense, *Adult English Two,* Units 9 and 10

PRESENT PERFECT CONTINUOUS TENSE

Circle the numbers in front of the correct completion for each sentence. Then go over the answers with the teacher.

A.   Look at sentence 4. The present continuous tense shows only that the action is happening right now. Which tense shows that the action began in the past *and* continues right now?

     1. past tense

     2. present perfect continuous tense

B.   Look at sentences,1, 7, and 9 above. The past tense shows that an action started in the past and finished in the past. Do present perfect continuous actions finish in the past?

     1. yes

     2. no

C.   Look at these two sets of sentences:

Present Perfect Tense	I have lived in three different countries.
Present Perfect Continuous Tense	I have been living here for three months.
Present Perfect Tense	I have met many Frenchmen.
Present Perfect Continuous Tense	I have been meeting a lot of Frenchmen.

*not usually used in continuous form.

Name _____ Date _____

Which tense brings the action closer to the present moment?

1. present perfect tense

2. present perfect continuous tense

ORAL PRACTICE

Work in pairs. Take turns making sentences using the present perfect continuous tense. The first person reads the sentence in the book and the cue words in parentheses. The second person says a present perfect continuous sentence. Use *for* with periods of time (*for three hours*) and *since* with exact times (*since* 3:00).

Example: 1. First Person: We are studying. (three hours)

Second Person: *we have been studying for three hours.*

2. Karen is trying on shoes.   (fifteen minutes)

3. The baby can walk now.   (two weeks)

4. Al is watching television.   (an hour)

5. Carol is cleaning the kitchen.   (1:00)

6. Bill is painting the hall.   (8:00)

7. Alice is doing homework.   (6:00)

8. Carol plays tennis every day now.   (April)

QUESTIONS AND ANSWERS

Work in groups of four or five. Take turns asking and answering questions about Picture 3 using the cue words below. Later write in the missing words.

Example: 1. (live)   Question: How long *have they been living* on the farm?

Answer: They *have been living* on the farm for ten years.

Name _____   Date _____

2. (do) What _____ _____ _____ _____ seven days a week?

3. (do) What _____ _____ _____ _____ for half an hour?

4. (do) What _____ Mr. Miller _____ _____ while he is sitting there?

5. (talk about) What _____ _____ _____ _____ about?

6. (wait for) Who _____ _____ _____ _____ for?

7. (want) What _____ Mrs. Miller _____ _____ for several weeks?

8. (wait) How long _____ _____ _____ _____ for the neighbors?

WRITING PRACTICE

There are eight pairs of sentences below. Combine each pair of sentences into one sentence using the present perfect continuous tense.

Example: 1. I am wearing my coat. I put it on half an hour ago.

I have been wearing my coat for half an hour.

2. The wind is blowing. It started this morning.

_____

3. Alice is dancing. She started at 7:00.

_____

4. My sister is helping me. She started to help me two hours ago.

_____

5. We are talking about school. We started to talk fifteen minutes ago.

_____

6. I'm repairing this radio. I started at 6:00.

_____

7. Karen is shopping. She started three hours ago.

_____

8. I am holding the baby. I picked him up ten minutes ago.

_____

READING PASSAGE

The Millers have been living in this house for 25 years. They moved to the farm right after they got married. They have two sons— Ken and Howard. The boys don't live on the farm any more. Ken wanted to go to college, and Howard wanted to get a job. So they moved to the city two years ago.

The Millers work hard. Mr. Miller often works from 6:00 A.M. until 9:00 at night. He has six employees, but sometimes he could use even more. When he is really busy, his wife helps him with the heavy work. She can drive a truck and even milk cows. She likes to be busy. When she has nothing to do, she sometimes feels lonely. She misses her sons.

The Millers don't have much time to relax. The farm is their whole life. They work seven days a week. The only fun they have is watching television and sometimes visiting neighbors. Lately they have been talking about selling the farm. They could use the money to travel and to buy a smaller place.

But Mr. Miller really wants to keep the farm. He says that they have put a lot of work into it. He also thinks that maybe one of the boys will decide to come back someday. And Mrs. Miller doesn't really want to live in another house. This one is full of good feelings for her. It has held 25 years of family life. The farm is a very important part of both their lives. It would be hard for them to leave it.

READING QUESTIONS

Complete the following sentences based on the story above.

Fact

1. The Miller boys have gone _____.

2. They went there because _____.

3. Mr. Miller often works _____.

Name _____ _Date_ _____

4. Sometimes Mrs. Miller feels _____ .

5. _____ work for Mr. Miller.

Inference

1. The Millers are about _____ old.

2. They have been married for _____ .

3. They enjoy _____ .

4. They will probably _____ .

5. The farm is _____ .

VOCABULARY PRACTICE

Fill in the blanks using the following eight words:

farm	cows	whole	decide
employees	lonely	fun	feelings

1. He pays his _____ ten dollars a day.

2. _____ give milk.

3. On Saturday night I go out and have _____ .

4. I can't _____ which car to buy.

5. I have good _____ about my friends.

6. You can find cows on a _____ .

7. Sometimes I feel sad and _____ .

8. Don't give me half a cup. Give me a _____ cup.

Name_____ Date _____

STRUCTURES

See **Special Uses of** *It,* page 16, for explanation and examples.

How long		have	they	been	living	there?
	They	have		been	living	there for two years.

What		has	she	been	doing?
	She	has		been	talking.

VOCABULARY

Nouns	*Verbs*	*Adjectives*	*Other*
block	decide	fun	lately
construction	notice	lonely	_____
cow	_____	whole	_____
distance	_____	_____	_____
employee	_____	_____	_____
farm	_____	_____	_____
feelings	_____	_____	_____
identification	_____	_____	_____
period	_____	_____	_____
porch	_____	_____	_____
soccer	_____	_____	_____
snow	_____	_____	_____
supervisior	_____	_____	_____
_____	_____	_____	_____

Name _____ *Date* _____

HOMEWORK

A. Review **Special Uses of** *It,* page 16. Memorize two examples of each type. Be ready to say the examples when the teacher calls on you during the next class.

B. Review the **Paraphrasing** section, page 17. On a separate sheet of paper, write out the ten paraphrases.

C. Review the present perfect continuous tense. Make up five questions to ask your classmates. See the **Questions and Answers** section, page 21. Be ready to ask and answer these questions during the next class.

D. Look at Picture 2. Write five present perfect continuous sentences to describe what the men in the picture have been doing lately.

LISTENING EXERCISE

The teacher will read the following sentences. Fill in the missing words.

1. Where _____ _____ been living?

2. What _____ _____ found?

3. How long have _____ _____ waiting?

4. What has he _____ _____?

5. Where _____ _____ gone?

6. What have _____ _____ looking for?

7. What has Carol _____ _____?

8. Where has Al _____ _____?

9. Who _____ _____ been visiting?

10. Have _____ _____ sitting here long?

Name _____ *Date* _____

26

Unit 3

PICTURE TO TALK ABOUT

Danny wanted to learn how to ski. The teacher will tell about Danny's first lesson. Repeat each sentence. Then say the sentences to another student. Later write in the missing words.

Arthur H. Bilsten, Colorado Department of Public Relations

PICTURE 4

Name _____ Date _____

1. Danny _____ _____ _____ him skiing.

2. Mrs. Jensen _____ _____ _____ a heavy coat.

At first Danny was a little scared.

3. Mr. Jensen _____ _____ _____ down a big hill.

4. He _____ _____ _____ down a small hill.

They skiied down the hill together.

5. Mr. Jensen _____ _____ _____ several times.

The boy didn't want to ski down by himself.

6. But Mr. Jensen _____ _____ _____ down alone.

When he finished, both father and son were proud.

CAUSATIVE WITH *HAVE*

	have/had/has	+ Person	+ Base Form	
Examples: Mrs. Jensen	had	Danny	wear	a heavy coat.
Mr. Jensen	had	Danny	practice	several times.
I	had	the barber	cut	my hair.
Karen	had	the dentist	check	her teeth.

The *have* causative is used when you are sure the person will do what you ask. It shows that no force or persuasion was necessary. The *have* causative is used when you pay a person to do something.

Name _____ Date _____

CAUSATIVE WITH *MAKE*

	make/made/makes	+ Person	+ Base Form	
Examples: Mr. Jensen	didn't make	him	go	down a big hill.
Mr. Jensen	made	Danny	go	down alone.
The police	made	me	move	my car.
Her father	made	her	do	her homework.

The *make* causative is used when you have to force a person to do something that they don't want to do.

CAUSATIVE WITH *GET*

	get/got/gets	+ Person	+ Infinitive	
Examples: Danny	got	his father	to take	him skiing.
He	got	Danny	to go	down alone.
I	got	my father	to give	me five dollars.
Karen	got	her sister	to clean	the house.

The *get* causative is used when you persuade or convince a person to do something.

CAUSATIVE PRACTICE

Work in pairs. Paraphrase the following sentences using causatives. Later write in the missing words.

Example: 1. (get) Danny asked to go skiing. Finally his father took him skiing.

Danny _____ ' _____ _____ him skiing.

2. (make)   I was very tired Saturday morning. My sister forced me to get up.

My sister _____ _____ _____ Saturday morning.

3. (have)   Mr. Jensen can't type. He asks his secretary to type his letters and she does.

Mr. Jensen _____ _____ _____ his letters.

4. (have)   Alice asked her brother to drive the car. He did.

Alice _____ _____ _____ the car.

5. (get)   Danny wanted to go home. He told his parents several times. Finally they went home.

Danny _____ _____ _____ home.

6. (make)   I wanted to go home at 3:00. The boss told me to work until 5:00.

The boss _____ _____ _____ until 5:00.

7. (have)   My telephone didn't work. I asked the repairman to repair it. He did.

I _____ _____ _____ my phone.

8. (make)   The medicine tasted terrible. The doctor forced me to take it.

The doctor _____ _____ _____ the medicine.

MORE CAUSATIVE PRACTICE

Work in groups of three or four. Take turns making causative sentences using items from the four columns. Be sure to use the base form with *make* and *have* and the infinitive with *get*.

Example: The boss made us work hard.

CHART 1

Column 1	Column 2	Column 3	Column 4
The police	got	us	(to) work hard
The boss			(to) stop the car
My sister	made	the workers	(to) buy a dictionary
My children	had	Alice	(to) help her
My parents		me	(to) paint my room
		her	
I			(to) buy ice-cream
The teacher			(to) take some medicine
The doctor			(to) study hard

WRITING PRACTICE

Complete the causative sentences below. Tell the truth about your life.

1. I got _____.

2. I made _____.

3. I had _____.

4. _____ got me _____.

5. _____ made me _____.

6. _____ had me _____.

USING TAG QUESTIONS

Look at Picture 2 on page 14 and review the conversation. Before Bill left for California, Larry asked him a lot of questions. Repeat each line of the dialog after the teacher. Then practice the dialog with another student. Later fill in the missing words.

Larry: You like to travel, _____ _____?

Bill: Yes, I do. You don't like to travel, _____ _____?

Larry: No, I don't. It will take two weeks to drive to California,

    _____ _____?

Bill: Yes, it will. I plan to visit a friend in Chicago.

Larry: You won't stay long, _____ _____?

Bill: No. Only one day. You told the California office who I am,

    _____ _____?

Larry: Yes, I did. They will be happy to see you.

Bill: Well, I'm ready to go now.

Larry: You didn't forget your bathing suit, _____ _____?

Bill: I didn't forget it. I hope I have time to use it.

Larry: Good luck, Bill.

Bill: Thanks. Good-bye Larry.

Note: When the main verb is affirmative, the tag is always negative.

When the main verb is negative, the tag is always affirmative.
The main verb and the tag are always the same tense.

PRACTICE WITH TAG QUESTIONS

Work in pairs. One person completes the question with a tag. The other person gives a yes or no answer.

Example: 1. First person: You drove to school, _____ _____?

    Second person: _____, _____ _____.

2. The teacher won't leave early, _____ _____?

3. You didn't open the window, _____ _____?

4. You don't smoke, _____ _____?

Name _____ Date _____

5. Class will start soon, _____ _____?

6. She swims very well, _____ _____?

7. Bill likes to travel, _____ _____?

8. You stayed home yesterday, _____ _____?

9. Larry doesn't go to movies, _____ _____?

10. Alice reads a lot, _____ _____?

TALK ABOUT YOURSELVES

Work in groups of four or five. Fill in the first blank in each question with the name of a student in the group. Then take turns asking and answering the questions. Later write in the missing words.

Example: 1. _____ doesn't smoke, _____?

_____.

2. _____ will cook dinner tonight, _____?

_____.

3. _____ is tall, _____?

_____.

4. _____ wasn't late to class today, _____?

_____.

5. _____ hasn't met the President, _____?

_____.

6. _____ won't be here tomorrow, _____?

_____.

*Name*_____ *Date* _____

7. _____ studies hard, _____?

_____.

8. _____ has lived here for more than a year, _____?

_____.

9. _____ wrote on the blackboard, _____?

_____.

10. _____ isn't very talkative, _____?

_____.

WRITING PRACTICE

Fill in the main verb in each question below. Then write a correct response.

1. Alice _____ yet, has she? _____.

2. She _____ either, did she? _____.

3. She _____ soon, won't she? _____.

4. She _____ near here, doesn't she? _____.

5. She _____ usually early, isn't she? _____.

6. She _____ yesterday, didn't she? _____.

7. You _____ her, will you? _____.

8. You _____ her telephone number, do you? _____.

READING PASSAGE

When Bill arrived in California, he went right to the company's main office in Los Angeles. There he met the West Coast managers. The words that they said were friendly, but their eyes weren't. Mr. Lewis asked Bill a lot of questions about construction work. He wanted to know how long Bill had been working. Mr. Caputo asked about his education. Bill answered all the questions, but the men just nodded. Bill didn't say anything else.

The next day Bill went out to the construction site. There he met the work crew. They were a lot friendlier than the office crew. After a fifteen-minute meeting, they all went to work. Bill spent the whole day at the site. He took time to talk to each man individually. They talked about the job, their families, and their future plans. As the men were leaving at 5:00, Bill heard one man say, "The new boss is going to be O.K."

After a week on the job, Bill called the New York office. Larry and Bill talked happily for fifteen minutes. Then there was a long silence.

Larry: Listen, Bill. There's a little problem in L.A.

Bill: On the construction site? With the work crew?

Larry: No, they're really happy with the work you're doing there. It's the office crew. They haven't said anything, but I think they're a little afraid of you. They may think that you want to take over.

Bill: How could they think that? I didn't say anything.

Larry: That's just it. You answered all their questions perfectly. But you didn't ask any questions yourself.

Bill: Yes, well I was a little nervous. I didn't open up to them very much.

Larry: I guess they thought you were a know-it-all.

Bill: Oh, boy! I'll have to do something about that. Thanks for telling me.

Larry: I know you. It'll be no problem. Take care, Bill.

Bill: Thanks, Larry. Good-bye.

READING QUESTIONS

Write T in front of true sentences and F in front of false ones.

Fact

_____ 1. The West Coast managers are in Los Angeles.

_____ 2. The managers asked Bill a lot of questions.

_____ 3. Bill asked the managers a lot of questions.

_____ 4. The work crew was friendlier than the office crew.

_____ 5. Bill talked to the work crew about their families.

Inference

_____ 1. The West Coast managers liked Bill.

_____ 2. Mr. Lewis was friendly.

_____ 3. The work crew liked Bill.

_____ 4. Larry was happy to talk with Bill.

_____ 5. Larry thinks Bill is a know-it-all.

WHEN DID IT HAPPEN?

Put a number one in front of the sentence that shows what happened first. Put a two in front of the second event, and so forth.

_____ Bill went to the main office.

_____ Bill went to the construction site.

_____ Bill said, "I was a little nervous."

_____ Larry said, "There's a little problem in L.A."

_____ Bill met the West Coast managers.

_____ Bill met the work crew.

_____ Bill and Larry talked happily.

_____ Mr. Lewis asked Bill a lot of questions.

Name _____ Date _____

_____ The work crew went home.

_____ Bill talked to each worker individually.

STRUCTURES

See **Causative with _Have_,** page 28, for explanation and examples.
See **Causative with _Make_,** page 29, for explanation and examples.
See **Causative with _Get_,** page 29, for explanation and examples.

You	're	early,	aren't you?
You	're not	late,	are you?
Alice	wrote	a letter,	didn't she?
You	didn't answer	the letter,	did you?
Bill	has left,		hasn't he?
Larry	hasn't arrived,		has he?

VOCABULARY

Nouns	_Verbs_	_Adjectives_	_Other_
barber	check	main	Good luck
bathing suit	force	proud	individually
coat	nod	terrible	perfectly
education	ski	_____	_____
hill	take over	_____	_____
ice cream	_____	_____	_____
medicine	_____	_____	_____
silence	_____	_____	_____
site	_____	_____	_____
skiing	_____	_____	_____
work crew	_____	_____	_____
_____	_____	_____	_____
_____	_____	_____	_____

Name _____ _Date_ _____

HOMEWORK

A. Be ready to answer using causative sentences during the next class.

1. Your rich uncle is visiting you for a week.
   What three things will you *get* him to do?
   Example: I *will get him to buy* me dinner.

2. Your young child has a bad cold.
   What three things will you *make* her do?

3. Your house needs some repairs. A carpenter is coming.
   What three things will you *have* him do?

B. Review Chart 1 on page 31. Write six causative sentences using the items in the chart.

1. _____.

2. _____.

3. _____.

4. _____.

5. _____.

6. _____.

C. Review the reading passage on page 35. Be ready to change each sentence in the first paragraph to a tag question.

Example: When Bill arrived in California, he went right to the main office in Los Angeles, *didn't he*?

D. Complete these tag questions.

1. You didn't swim yesterday, _____?

2. You play tennis, _____?

Name _____ Date _____

3. He hasn't met you, _____?

4. Alice was ready, _____?

5. Bill didn't call, _____?

6. She has finished it, _____?

7. They're funny, _____?

8. You were busy last night, _____?

LISTENING EXERCISE

The teacher will read some tag questions. Write the tags only.

1.   2.

3.   4.

5.   6.

7.   8.

9.   10.

Unit 4

A MAP TO TALK ABOUT

On the map locate the cities where Beverly, Marta, Jack, and Alfredo live. The teacher will describe the location of each place using *in, on,* and *at.* Repeat each sentence. Then say the sentences to another student. Later write in the missing words.

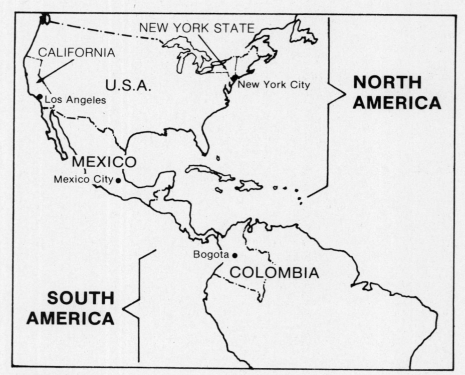

NEW YORK STATE

CALIFORNIA

U.S.A.

New York City

NORTH
AMERICA

Los Angeles

MEXICO

Mexico City

Bogota

COLOMBIA

SOUTH
AMERICA

PICTURE 5

Name _____ Date _____

The United States is _____ North America.   (continent)

California is _____ the United States.   (country)

Los Angeles is _____ California.   (state)

Beverly lives _____ Los Angeles.   (city)

She lives _____ Fulton Street.   (street)

She lives _____ 231 Fulton Street.   (house number)

Colombia is _____ South America.   (continent)

Bogotá is _____ Colombia.   (country)

Marta lives _____ Bogotá.   (city)

She lives _____ Station Street.   (street)

She lives _____ 45 Station Street.   (house number)

FILL-INS

Fill in other examples of each item below.

Continents: _Africa_____, _____, _____

Countries: _Columbia___, _____, _____

States: _California_, _____, _____

Cities: _Paris_____, _____, _____

Streets: _Fifth Ave_, _____, _____

House Numbers: 650 Fifth Ave_____, _____

Name _____ *Date* _____

USING *IN, ON,* AND *AT* WITH PLACES

Review the items under Picture 5 (continent, country, state, city, street, and house number).

1. Which item describes the smallest area? _____

   Which word (*in, on,* or *at*) goes with that item? _____

2. Which item describes a bigger area? _____

   Which word (*in, on,* or *at*) goes with that item? _____

3. Which four items describe large areas? _____

   _____

   _____

   _____

   Which word (*in, on,* or *at*) goes with those four items? _____

4. So _____ goes with the smallest place, _____ goes with a bigger

   place, and _____ goes with the four biggest places.

PRACTICE *IN, ON,* AND *AT* WITH PLACES

Work in pairs. Take turns making sentences like those under Picture 5. Use Jack's address and Alfredo's address for this practice.

Example: First person: The United States is in North America.

Other person: New York State is in the United States.

TALK ABOUT YOURSELVES

Work in groups of four or five. Take turns telling where a friend, a relative, or a famous person lives. Use the continent, the country, the state (if possible), the city, the street, and the house number.

Example: My sister is working *in* the United States.
The United States is *in* North America.
She lives *in* Florida.

She works *in* Miami.
She lives *on* 17th Avenue (Northwest).
She lives *at* 250 17th Avenue (Northwest).

WRITING PRACTICE

Use the patterns from the **Talk About Yourselves** exercise. Write a six-sentence description of where a friend lives.

1. _____.

2. _____.

3. _____.

4. _____.

5. _____.

6. _____.

A DIAGRAM TO TALK ABOUT

Look over the diagram on page 44. The teacher will describe when each event happened using *in, on,* and *at.* Repeat each sentence. Then say the sentence to another student. Later write in the missing words.

Name _____ *Date* _____

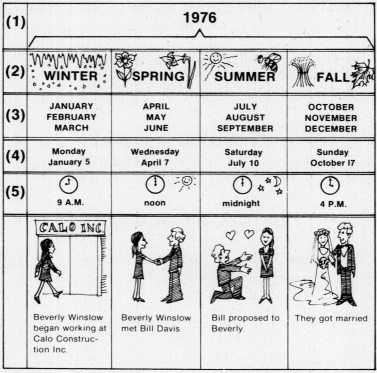

PICTURE 6

Beverly began working _____ 1976.   (year)

She began _____ the winter.   (season)

She started _____ January.   (month)

She started work _____ January 5.   (date)

(She started work _____ Monday, January 5.)   (day of the week)

*She came to work _____ 9 A.M.   (time of day)

Beverly also met Bill _____ 1976.   (year)

They met _____ the spring.   (season)

She met him _____ April.   (month)

　　　*See *Adult English One,* Units 6 and 8.

Name _____ *Date* _____

They met _____ April 7.   (date)

(They met _____ Wednesday, April 7.)   (day of the week)

*They met _____ noon.   (time of day)

USING *IN, ON,* AND *AT* WITH TIME

Review the items under Picture 6 (year, season, month, date, day of the week, and time of day).

1. Which item describes the most exact time? _____

   Which word (*in, on,* or *at*) goes with that item? _____

2. Which two items describe a longer period of time? _____

   _____

   Which word (*in, on,* or *at*) goes with these two items? _____

3. Which three items describe the longest period of time? _____

   _____

   _____

   Which word (*in, on,* or *at*) goes with these three items? _____

4. So, _____ goes with the most exact time; _____ goes with longer periods of time; and _____ goes with the three longest periods of time.

5. With places *and* with times, _____ goes with the biggest and longest; _____ goes with the middle items; and _____ goes with the smallest and most exact items.

   *See *Adult English One,* Units 6 and 8.

Name_____ Date _____

PRACTICE *IN, ON,* AND *AT* WITH TIMES

Work in pairs. Take turns making sentences like those under Picture 6. Use Bill's proposal and their marriage for this practice.

Example: First person: Bill proposed in 1976.

                Other person: He proposed in the summer.

TALK ABOUT YOURSELVES

Work in groups of four or five. Take turns telling about important events in your life. Tell when the event happened using year, season, month, day, date, and time.

Example: I arrived in this country *in* 1977.
             I came *in* winter.
             I arrived *in* February.
             I arrived *on* Monday, February 14.
             My plane arrived *at* 8 A.M.

WRITING PRACTICE

Use the patterns from the **Talk About Yourselves** exercise. Write a six-sentence description of an important event in your life.

1. _____ .

2. _____ .

3. _____ .

4. _____ .

5. _____ .

6. _____ .

Name _____ *Date* _____

Bill had been working in Los Angeles for several weeks. The people in the office had begun to feel comfortable with him. One day Mr. Caputo invited Bill to lunch. They were just leaving the building when they passed Beverly Winslow. She was coming back from an early lunch. "Who was that?" asked Bill. "Ms Winslow," answered Mr. Caputo. "She's been working in the accounting department for three months. Doing a good job, too."

Later that afternoon Bill stopped by the accounting department. He saw Ms Winslow at her desk by the window. She looked up and smiled as he crossed the room toward her.

Bill: Hello, Ms Winslow.
Beverly: I'm Beverly. You're Bill Davis, aren't you?
Bill: How did you know?
Beverly: I asked Mr. Caputo after he came back from lunch.
Bill: Oh.
Beverly: Do you want to have lunch together tomorrow?

Bill was a little surprised, but very pleased. They had lunch together the next day, and the next, and the next. On Saturday they drove to the mountains, and on Sunday to the ocean. By Monday morning Bill was sure he had found *the* woman for him. And Beverly was sure of her feelings, too.

But there was one problem. Bill had to go back to New York. Beverly had to stay in Los Angeles. She was beginning to move up in Calo, Inc. After just three months, she had received a raise. Even the president of the company knew who she was. She had a good future with Calo in Los Angeles. And her family was there.

One evening in the middle of June, Bill and Beverly discussed their future.

Bill: I have to go back to New York next week.
Beverly: I know. When will we see each other again?
Bill: Can you get some vacation next month? Will you visit me then?
Beverly: Well, I'll sure try. But what do we do until then?
Bill: I know what I'll be doing—thinking about you.

READING QUESTIONS

Fact

Write T in front of true sentences and F in front of false ones.

_____ 1. Beverly has been with Calo for three years.

Name _____ *Date* _____

47

_____ 2. Beverly asked Mr. Caputo Bill's name.

_____ 3. Beverly and Bill had lunch together three times the week they met.

_____ 4. Bill was staying in Los Angeles for a year.

_____ 5. Beverly will try to go to New York in July.

Inference

_____ 1. Mr. Caputo is Bill's boss.

_____ 2. After lunch Beverly tried to find Bill.

_____ 3. Beverly wanted to leave her job.

_____ 4. The first time they met, Beverly and Bill liked each other.

_____ 5. Bill will miss Beverly when he is in New York.

WHEN DID IT HAPPEN?

Put a number one in front of the sentence that shows what happened first. Put a two in front of the second event, and so forth.

_____ Beverly asked Mr. Caputo Bill's name.

_____ Beverly and Bill went to the mountains.

_____ Bill and Mr. Caputo passed Beverly.

_____ Bill knew Beverly was _the_ woman for him.

_____ Mr. Caputo invited Bill to lunch.

_____ Bill had been working in Los Angeles for three months.

_____ Beverly and Bill plan to meet in New York.

Name _____ _Date_ _____

_____ Beverly says that she can't leave her job.

_____ Beverly and Bill had lunch together for the first time.

_____ Bill visited Beverly for the first time.

STRUCTURES

in	continents, countries, states, cities
on	streets
at	house numbers

See page 41 for examples.

in	years, months
on	dates, days of the week
at	times of the day

See page 44 for examples.

VOCABULARY

Nouns	*Verbs*	*Adjectives*	*Other*
accounting	begin	_____	_____
company	cross		
continent	discuss	_____	_____
fall	invite		
middle	move up	_____	_____
mountains	pass		
ocean	_____	_____	_____
spring			
state	_____	_____	_____
_____	_____	_____	_____

Name _____ *Date* _____

HOMEWORK

A. Be prepared to make statements like those under Picture 5 using *in, on,* and *at* with places. Be ready to talk about the following:

Kimiko Hiri   Mohamad Rasai
36 Talaka Street   420 Akmed Avenue
Tokyo, Japan   Cairo, Egypt

B. Write out the statements for one of the names above.

C. Be prepared to tell when your country became independent using *in, on,* and *at* with times.

D. Review the reading passage on page 47. What do you think will happen to Bill and Beverly? Write several sentences that will complete the story.

_____

_____

_____

_____

_____

_____

LISTENING EXERCISE

The teacher will read some sentences. Write the second word you hear.

1.   2.

3.   4.

5.   6.

7.   8.

9.   10.

Name _____ *Date* _____

Unit 5

PICTURE TO TALK ABOUT

Disneyland is a big amusement park in California. While Bill was working in California, he visited the park. Now he is showing his father this picture of a parade at Disneyland. The teacher will read the dialog between Bill and his father. Repeat each sentence. Then practice the dialog with another student. Later write in the missing words.

Walt Disney Productions

PICTURE 7

Name_____ Date_____

Father: _____ is watching the parade.

Bill: _____ is bored.

Father: Is _____ taking a picture?

Bill: Sure. Look over there. _____ is taking a picture.

Bill: _____ at Disneyland is beautiful!

Father: Is _____ old and dirty?

Bill: No. _____ is old and dirty.

And _____ is happening all the time.

Bill: People come from _____ to see Disneyland.

There is _____ nicer for a vacation.

Father: Are you going _____ on your vacation?

Bill: Sure, I'm going _____—to Disneyland.

PATTERNS WITH *EVERY-, NO-, ANY-,* AND *SOME-*

Review the fill-ins under Picture 7. Then complete the three sections below. Write each of the four words at the top of the section in the correct blank.

Everyone, No One, Anyone, Someone

_____ = one person (used in questions and negative statements)

_____ = one person (used in affirmative statements)

_____ = no people

_____ = all the people

Everything, Nothing, Anything, Something

_____ = one item (used in questions and negative statements)

_____ = all items

Name _____ *Date* _____

_____ = one item (used in affirmative statements)

_____ = not one item

Everywhere, Nowhere, Anywhere, Somewhere

_____ = one place (used in affirmative statements)

_____ = all places

_____ = not one place

_____ = one place (used in questions and negative statements)

PRACTICE WITH EVERY-, NO-, ANY-, AND SOME-

Work in pairs. The dialog on the right paraphrases the one on the left. First practice saying the dialog on the left. Be sure you understand each line. Then work together to fill in the missing words in the right-hand dialog. Use the twelve words from the **Patterns** exercise. Then practice saying the right-hand dialog. Repeat these steps for all three sections.

Note: These twelve words are followed by singular (not plural) verbs.

Section One

A: All the students came to school.   _____ came to school.

B. Did any student forget the homework?   Did _____ forget the homework?

A: Yes, one student forgot it.   Yes, _____ forgot it.

But all the students remembered the book.   But _____ remembered the book.

Section Two

A: Did you bring all your books?   Do you have _____?

B: No. I forgot one.   No. I forgot _____.

Name _____ Date _____

A: But you never forget things!

But you never forget _____!

B: Yes, I do. Everyone makes mistakes.

Yes, I do. _____ is perfect.

Section Three

A: Let's visit another part of the city.

Let's go _____.

B: No. I want to stay home.

I don't want to go _____.

I've visited every part of the city.

I've been _____ in the city.

A: But we'll be bored at home.

But there's _____ to do at home.

B: We'll amuse ourselves.

We'll find _____ to do.

DIALOGS WITH *EVERY-, NO-, ANY-,* **AND** *SOME-*

Work in groups of four or five. First work together to fill in the missing words in Section One. Then take turns reading the dialog to the rest of the group. Correct each other's errors. Repeat these steps for all three sections.

Section One

A: Did you bring _____ to eat?

B: No. Let's go _____ for lunch.

A: Shall we ask _____ to go with us?

B: It's too late. _____ has gone already.

Section Two

A: I have _____ to tell you.

_____ took my wallet.

I can't find it _____.

I've looked _____.

Name _____ Date _____

B: Did you look on the floor by your desk?

A: Oh, there it is!

Section Three

A:. I'm so lonely. I have _____ to do after school.

I have _____ to go.

_____ ever calls me up.

B. Why don't you do something about it?

A: What can I do? Maybe tomorrow _____ will notice me.

WRITING PRACTICE

Paraphrase the following sentences.

Example: I don't know one person in Boston.

I don't know anyone in Boston.

1. I want to talk with you.

   I have _____ to tell you.

2. Bill sold all the items in his apartment.

   _____.

3. Do you know a person in New York?

   _____.

4. There isn't a place colder than Alaska.

   _____ colder than Alaska.

5. I saw a person driving your car.

   _____.

6. Did you take a trip last weekend?

   Did you go _____?

7. Bill didn't say a word.

   Bill said _____.

8. People from every country of the world love ice-cream.

   _____.

PICTURE TO TALK ABOUT

The ten sentences describe Picture 8. Each sentence contains several adjectives plus a noun. Repeat each sentence. Then say the sentences to another student. Later write in the missing words.

PICTURE 8

1. _____ _____ _____ trees are short.

2. _____ _____ _____ trees are tall.

3. _____ _____ _____ trees are short.

4. In front of the house is _____ _____ _____ car.

5. Beside it is _____ _____ _____ man.

6. Beside him is _____ _____ _____ man.

7. The young man is wearing _____ _____ _____ shirt.

8. He has _____ _____ pants.

9. He's wearing _____ _____ shoes.

10. He's carrying _____ _____ _____ bag.

ORDER OF ADJECTIVES BEFORE A NOUN

When two or three adjectives come right before a noun, there is only one correct order for the adjectives.*

Example: Right—*The last three* trees are short.

Wrong—*The three last* trees are short.

Wrong—*Last the three* trees are short.

Chart 1 shows seven types of adjectives in the correct order. One example of each type has been written in. Look at the sentences under Picture 8. Copy the rest of the adjectives in the correct column below.

*You *almost never* use more than three adjectives before a noun.

Name_____ Date _____

CHART 1

The/A +	Ordinal Number, etc. +	Cardinal Number +	Size +	Age +	Color +	Material +	Noun
The	first	two	big	new	blue	cotton	trees
							man
							shirt
							car
							bag
							etc.

PRACTICE THE ORDER OF ADJECTIVES

Take turns making sentences using the noun and three adjectives after each number.

Example: 1. bag — red   the   big

The big red bag is mine. (Give me the big red bag.)

2. problems — two   the   first

3. shirt — cotton   white   a

4. car — new   a   blue

5. bag — leather   brown   a

6. children — five   little   the

7. woman — old   a   fat

8. house — white   big   second

Name _____ Date _____

MORE PRACTICE WITH THE ORDER OF ADJECTIVES

Work in groups of four or five. Each person writes three sentences about items in the room using the pattern adjective + adjective + adjective + noun. Then take turns reading the sentences and correcting each other. Use the **Order of Adjectives** chart.

Examples: Luis is wearing *a white cotton* shirt.

The teacher has *a big black* book.

There are *two small wooden* tables in the corner.

WRITING PRACTICE

The teacher will place six items in the front of the room and write the name of each on the blackboard. Then students will suggest adjectives to describe each item, and the teacher will write these on the board. After that, write one sentence for each item using the pattern adjective + adjective + adjective + noun.

1. _____.

2. _____.

3. _____.

4. _____.

5. _____.

6. _____.

READING PASSAGE

Look at Picture 3 on page 19 and review the **Reading Passage** on page 23.

Last summer Ken and Howard gave their parents a wonderful present. Mr. and Mrs. Miller had lived on the farm for ten years. They hadn't been away from it for more than a day. So last summer Ken and Howard offered to run the farm for two weeks. They told their parents to take a trip somewhere. The boys didn't have to offer twice. A week later Mr. and Mrs. Miller were in California.

Name _____ *Date* _____

They spent the first three days in Los Angeles. Mrs. Miller wanted to see how they make television programs. So they spent one day at the T.V. studios. They spent another day in Hollywood seeing how they make movies. The Millers hoped to meet a movie star or two, but they didn't see anyone famous. The third day they took a bus tour around Los Angeles. They saw a lot of theaters, a couple of colleges, and some very beautiful homes.

The fourth day they drove to Disneyland. Some of their Vermont friends had been there before. The Millers had heard a lot about it. It was even better than they had hoped. There were rides and shows and movies. Something was happening every minute. The best part was the parade. They had nothing like that back in Vermont.

The second week the Millers relaxed. They found a quiet hotel in a town on the ocean. For six days they watched television, read the papers, and took long walks by the water. It was the first time in ten years that they could sit back and do nothing. And they enjoyed it.

"You know," Mr. Miller said on the way home in the plane, "I could learn to be lazy if I tried." "Me too," said Mrs. Miller. "And it wouldn't take much practice either."

READING QUESTIONS

Fact

Complete the following sentences using the facts in the story.

1. Ken and Howard offered _____.

2. They told their parents _____.

3. A week later _____.

4. The first three days _____.

5. They hoped to meet _____.

6. The fourth day _____.

7. Disneyland was _____.

8. The second week _____.

Name _____ *Date* _____

9. They found _____.

10. Mr. Miller said that he could learn _____.

MAIN IDEA

Pick out the main idea of each paragraph by circling (a), (b), or (c).

Example: Paragraph One

    (a) The Millers went to California.

    (b) Ken and Howard helped their parents take a vacation.

    (c) The Millers had lived on the farm for ten years.

Paragraph Two

(a) The Millers saw a lot in Los Angeles.

(b) The Millers didn't see anyone famous.

(c) Mrs. Miller saw how they make T.V. shows.

Paragraph Three

(a) The Millers' friends had liked Disneyland.

(b) The fourth day they drove to Disneyland.

(c) The Millers had three wonderful days at Disneyland.

Paragraph Four

(a) Finally the Millers relaxed.

(b) They took walks by the ocean.

(c) They watched television.

STRUCTURES

Everyone	No one	Anyone	Someone
Everything	Nothing	Anything	Something
Everywhere	Nowhere	Anywhere	Somewhere

See page 52 for examples of *every-*, *no-*, *any-*, and *some-* words. See page 52 and 53 for explanations of these words.

Name _____ Date _____

See Chart 1, page 58, for an explanation and some examples of the **Order of Adjectives.**

VOCABULARY

Nouns	Verbs	Adjectives	Other
college	amuse	beautiful	_____
floor	enjoy	blue	_____
item	offer	bored	_____
movie star	_____	brown	_____
parade	_____	cotton	_____
program	_____	denim	_____
studio	_____	dirty	_____
theater	_____	green	_____
tour	_____	leather	_____
weekend	_____	nice	_____
_____	_____	plastic	_____
_____	_____	wonderful	_____
_____	_____	_____	_____
_____	_____	_____	_____

HOMEWORK

A. Memorize one or two of the dialogs on page 54. Be ready to perform either role in class without looking at the book.

B. Paraphrase the following sentences using *every-, no-, any-,* and *some-* words.

Name _____ Date _____

1. We never *leave the house* on weekends.

   _____.

2. *Not one person* knew the teacher's name.

   _____.

3. The baby wants *food or milk or a toy*.

   _____.

4. Trees grow *in all the countries* in Europe.

   _____.

5. Don't say *one word*!

   _____!

C. Bring five items to class. They can include clothes, books, toys, etc. Be ready to describe each one using the pattern adjective + adjective + adjective + noun.

D. Write sentences using the noun and three adjectives after each number.

   1. bags — new   leather   two

      _____.

   2. windows — first   the   three

      _____.

   3. wallet — plastic   brown   new

      _____.

4. car — blue   new   a

_____.

5. hat — denim   big   blue

_____.

LISTENING EXERCISE

Fill in the missing words.

1. Do you have _____ to go?

2. Yes, I have _____ to go.

3. Have you seen _____?

4. No. _____ has passed.

5. There are _____ _____ _____ houses over there.

6. _____ _____ _____ books are mine.

7. I like your _____ _____ _____ pants.

8. Talk to _____ _____ _____ woman.

9. Bill has _____ _____ _____ dog.

10. Wear your _____ _____ _____ coat.

Name_____ Date _____

Unit 6

PICTURE TO TALK ABOUT

These men work in a clothing factory. The teacher will describe the picture using the words *each, every,* and *all.* Repeat each sentence. Then say the sentences to another student. Later write in the missing words.

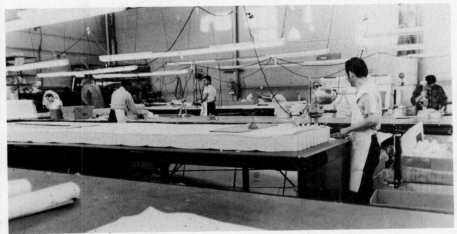

JUSTICE—ILGWU Photo

PICTURE 9

1. _____ _____ _____ are working hard.

2. _____ _____ has a different job.

Name _____ *Date* _____

3. Sometimes they help _____ _____.

4. _____ _____ the employees make clothes. Some work

in the office.

*5. _____ _____ need time to relax.

6. _____ _____ gets a two-week vacation.

*Universal statement = all employees in all businesses everywhere.

DIALOG

Mrs. Kwan is talking to the family doctor about her children. Notice the use of *each, every,* and *all* in the dialog. Repeat each line after the teacher. Then practice the dialog with another student.

Doctor: *All children* need to play outdoors.
Mrs. Kwan: Do they need exercise *every day*?
Doctor: Certainly. And team games are best. That way *all the children* get a lot of exercise.
Mrs. Kwan: But *not all* children like team games. Sometimes my children don't want to play with *each other.*
Doctor: I understand. *Each child* is different. You have to notice individual needs.

EACH, EVERY, AND ALL

Go over the two columns with the teacher. Be sure you understand each item. Each letter in Column 2 is followed by a description. Match the descriptions in Column 2 with the examples in Column 1. One letter will be used twice. Ask the teacher to check your work.

Column 1

_____ 1. *Each* + Singular Noun
Each man has a different job.

_____ 2. *Each Other*
Sometimes they help *each other.*

Column 2

A. Part of the group
B. Universal statement
C. Individual members of a group—emphasizes single members
D. Individual members of a group—emphasizes whole group
E. Two or more people doing something together

Name _____ Date _____

_____ 3. *Every* + Singular Noun

Every employee gets a two-week vacation.

_____ 4. *All* + *The* + Plural Noun

All the men are working hard.

_____ 5. *All* + Plural Noun

All workers need to relax.

_____ 6. *Not* + *All* + Plural Noun

Not all employees make clothes.

PRACTICE *EACH, EVERY,* AND *ALL*

Work in pairs. Take turns saying the sentences to each other filling in the words *each, every,* and *all.* Some sentences can be correctly completed two ways.

Example: 1. I learn something new ___*every*___ day.
                                    (*each*)

2. _____ the questions were easy.

3. _____ questions had three answers.

4. I answered _____ question carefully.

5. _____ parents want their children to get a good education.

6. _____ children in the United States have to go to school.

7. But not _____ children like to go to school.

8. Some children never listen. They're always talking with

_____ other.

Name _____ Date _____

TALK ABOUT PICTURE 9

Work in groups of four or five. Take turns using the lists below to make sentences about Picture 9. Combine one item form Column 1 and one item from Column 2.

Examples: 1. Each employee . . .

Each employee has a different job.

Each employee needs time to relax.

Column 1   Column 2

1. Each employee . . .   A. go home at 5:00.
                                  B. workers love vacations.
                                  C. has a different job.
2. All the employees . . .   D. They often help . . .
                                  E. employees make money.
3. . . . each other.   F. are working hard.
                                  G. needs time to relax.
4. Every worker . . .   H. The men talk to . . .

5. Not all the men . . .

6. All . . .

WRITING PRACTICE

Use the sentence parts from the last exercise. Complete the six Column 1 sentences in the blanks below.

1. _____ .

2. _____ .

3. _____ .

4. _____ .

5. _____ .

6. _____ .

Name _____ *Date* _____

On March 11, 1911 there was a very bad fire in a New York City clothing factory. The main door was locked and the fire escape was broken. One hundred and forty-six people died in that fire. Most of them were young girls. Many of the girls died jumping from open windows. Newspapers told the terrible story all over the country. People began to get angry about working conditions.

After the fire, working conditions began to get better. The government made some new laws. The workers began to join unions. A single employee could not change anything. But when thousands of employees got together, they were very strong. And many of those old unions are still strong today.

READING QUESTIONS

Write T in front of true sentences and F in front of false ones.

Fact

_____ 1. The men in the picture work forty hours a week.

_____ 2. Factories have always had good working conditions.

_____ 3. Around 1900 employees often worked seven days a week.

_____ 4. Many children used to work in factories.

_____ 5. Many of the old unions are still strong today.

Inference

_____ 1. The men in the picture work seven days a week.

_____ 2. Factory workers used to make so little money that the whole family needed to work.

_____ 3. Work rooms used to be uncomfortable.

_____ 4. In 1900 most factory workers got good medical care.

_____ 5. Unions have helped make working conditions better.

Name _____ *Date* _____

MAIN IDEA

Pick out the main idea of each paragraph by circling (a), (b), or (c).

Paragraph One

(a) The room is bright and sunny.

(b) The men get an hour for lunch.

(c) The men in the picture have good working conditions.

Paragraph Two

(a) Workers made little money in 1900.

(b) Working conditions were very bad in 1900.

(c) Whole families worked in factories.

Paragraph Three

(a) The fire escape was broken.

(b) There was a terrible fire in 1911.

(c) The main door was locked.

Paragraph Four

(a) Working conditions changed after the fire.

(b) A single employee is not very strong.

(c) People began to get angry.

STRUCTURES

See page 66 and 67 for explanation and examples of *each, every,* and *all.* See page 70 for explanation and examples of *either . . . or, neither . . . nor,* and *both . . . and.*

VOCABULARY

Nouns

conditions	fire escape	law	outdoors
cousin	government	meat	union
elephant	(first) grade	nurse	_____

Name _____ *Date* _____

Verbs	Adjectives	Other
die	angry	around
join	bright	certainly
lock	Chinese	_____
take a break	Japanese	_____
_____	_____	_____
_____	_____	_____

HOMEWORK

A. Review the *Each, Every,* and *All* section on page 66. Be ready to make original sentences for each of the six patterns. Think of sentences that describe real situations in your life.

B. Review the **Practice *Each, Every,* and *All*** section on page 67. Write out the eight sentences on a separate sheet of paper, filling in the missing words.

C. Be ready to answer these questions in class using *either . . . or, neither . . . nor,* and *both . . . and.*

    1. Are elephants small and thin?

    2. Who do you call when you feel sick?

    3. What do you drink in the morning?

    4. Do you wear a coat when it's cold?

    5. Do you like sugar in your coffee?

    6. When do you take a shower?

D. Review the **Questions and Answers** section on page 70. Write the answers to the eight questions below.

    1. _____.

    2. _____.

Name _____ *Date* _____

3. _____ .

4. _____ .

5. _____ .

6. _____ .

7. _____ .

8. _____ .

LISTENING EXERCISE

Fill in the missing words.

1. _____ three _____ four.

2. We've known _____ _____ for years.

3. _____ tall _____ fat.

4. _____ sunny _____ warm.

5. _____ _____ like fish.

6. _____ _____ _____ were late.

7. _____ Jim _____ Al.

8. _____ _____ leaves are green.

9. They love _____ _____ .

10. _____ flat _____ long.

Unit 7

PICTURES TO TALK ABOUT

These two pictures show the offices of Landmarks Incorporated. Picture 10 shows what the buildings looked like before repairs, and Picture 11 shows them after repairs. Repeat each sentence. Then practice saying the sentences to another student. Later write in the missing words.

Philadelphia Redevelopment Authority Photograph

PICTURE 10

Philadelphia Redevelopment Authority Photograph

PICTURE 11

Name _____ *Date* _____

In 1960 Landmarks Incorporated bought the buildings.

At the time they bought the buildings, no one _____ _____ in

them for ten years.

Some boys _____ _____ most of the windows.

Someone _____ _____ the first floor windows with wood.

Landmarks Incorporated finished repairing the buildings by 1964.

At the time Picture 11 was taken, they _____ _____ both

buildings.

But they _____ _____ in yet.

Also, someone _____ _____ a new building behind them.

PAST PERFECT TENSE

1. The past perfect tense uses _____ plus the past participle.
   See *Adult English Two,* Appendix 1, for a list of irregular past
   participles.

2. The past perfect tense is used to describe several events that happened
   in the past. The actions described in past perfect tense happened

   _____ the events described in past tense.

Look at the time line below:

1950-1960	4. July 10, 1960 *I took Picture 10.*	1960-1964	8. September 10, 1964 *I took Picture 11.*
1. No one *had lived* there.		5. They *had repaired* the building.	
2. Someone *had broken* the windows.		6. They *hadn't moved* in yet.	
3. Someone *had covered* the windows.		7. Someone *had built* a tall building.	

Name _____ Date _____

3. Sentences 1, 2, and 3 describe events that happened _____ the events in sentence 4.

4. Sentences 5, 6, and 7 describe events that happened _____ the events in sentence 8.

PRACTICE THE PAST PERFECT

Work in pairs. The events in sentences 1, 2, and 3 happened before the one in sentence 4. The events in sentences 5, 6, and 7 happened before the one in sentence 8. Fill in the blanks using past perfect tense. Then take turns reading the whole exercise to each other.

1. (to be)   Bill _____ _____ in New York for several months when he went to California.

2. (to meet) He _____ _____ Larry.

3. (to meet) He _____ *n't* _____ Mr. Caupto.

4. (to go)   Bill *went* to California in January.

5. (to work) He _____ _____ in California for six months when he returned to New York.

6. (to call) He _____ _____ Larry several times before he came back.

7. (to meet) Bill _____ _____ Beverly before he left California.

8. (to return) Bill *returned* to New York in June.

MORE PAST PERFECT PRACTICE

Work in groups of four or five. Take turns combining each pair of sentences into a single sentence. Use the past perfect tense to show which event happened first.

Example: 1. Howard *lived* on the farm for 18 years. Then he *moved* to the city.

Howard *had lived on the farm* when *he moved*. *for 18 years* *to the city*

Name _____ Date _____

2. I *studied* for two weeks. Then I *took* the exam.

I _____ when _____.

3. Bill *met* Mr. Caputo. Then he *called* Larry.

Bill _____ when _____.

4. Beverly *didn't see* Bill for two months. Then she *visited* him.

Beverly _____ when _____.

5. Alice *smoked* for ten years. Then she *stopped*.

Alice _____ when _____.

6. Luis *didn't speak* to anyone. Then he *left*.

Luis _____ when _____.

7. Ken *was* away for two years. Then he *returned*.

Ken _____ when _____.

8. I *had* my television for three years. Then I *sold* it.

I _____ when _____.

WRITING PRACTICE

Complete these sentences using the past perfect tense.

Example: 1. (listen) *Bill hAd ListeneD to the rADio* when
he turned it off.   *for An hour.*

2. (finish) _____ when the phone rang.

3. (live) _____ when
she returned to her country.

Name _____ *Date* _____

4. (work) _____ when they retired.

5. (stand) _____ when I finally found a seat.

6. (sleep) _____ when he woke up.

REPORTED SPEECH

Charlie's sister called him yesterday. Later Charlie told his wife, Pat, about the phone call. The original dialog is on the left. The reported dialog is on the right. Repeat the reported dialog. Then say it to another student. Later write in the missing words.

Original

Reported Speech

Ellen: Hello, Charlie. How are you?

Charlie: Fine.

1. Ellen: I*'m* very busy at work.

1. Ellen said that she _____ very busy at work.

2. The family *is* fine.

2. She said that the family _____ fine.

3. I *am planning* to visit Chicago.

3. She said that she _____ to visit Chicago.

4. Al *is coming,* too.

4. She said that Al _____, too.

5. He *wants* to see Chicago.

5. She said that he _____ to see Chicago.

6. We *need* a place to stay.

6. She said that they _____ a place to stay.

Charlie: You can stay with us.

WHAT HAPPENS IN REPORTED SPEECH?

Look at the last exercise and fill in the missing words following.

Name _____ *Date* _____

1. *Am* became _____.

2. *Is* became _____.

3. *Am planning* became _____.

4. *Is coming* became _____.

5. *Wants* became _____.

6. *Need* became _____.

7. Present tense became _____ tense.

8. Present continuous tense became _____ tense.

PRACTICE REPORTED SPEECH

Work in pairs. Change the following sentences to reported speech using the words *She said that . . .*

Example: 1. The weather is fine.

She said that the weather was fine.

2. The children are happy.

3. Billy is learning to play football.

4. Karen is studying French.

5. I hope to sell my old car.

6. I want to buy a new one.

MORE REPORTED SPEECH

Charlie wrote a letter to his sister, Ellen. The original letter is on the left. Use reported speech to tell another person what was in the letter. First repeat the reported speech. Then say each sentence to another student. Later write in the missing words.

Name _____ *Date* _____

Original	Reported Speech
Dear Ellen,	
1. I *have thought* about you a lot.	1. Charlie said that he _____ about her a lot.
2. I *was* worried.	2. He said that he _____ worried.
3. I *thought* you might be sick.	3. He said that he _____ she might be sick.
4. I *was* happy to talk with you.	4. He said he _____ happy to talk with her.
You must stay at our house.	
5. Pat *has started* to make plans already.	5. He said that Pat _____ to make plans already.
6. She *cleaned* the guest room on Saturday.	6. He said that she _____ the guest room on Saturday.

WHAT HAPPENS IN REPORTED SPEECH?

Look at the last exercise and fill in the missing words below.

1. *Was* became _____.

2. *Thought* became _____.

3. *Cleaned* became _____.

4. *Have thought* became _____.

5. *Has started* became _____.

6. Past tense became _____ tense.

7. Present perfect tense became _____ tense.

Name _____ Date _____

MORE REPORTED SPEECH PRACTICE

Work in pairs. Change the following sentences to reported speech using the words *He said that . . .*

Example: 1. We found a new house.

   He said that they had found a new house.

2. We bought it on Monday.

3. We were happy with the price.

4. Pat wasn't happy with the walls.

5. She has painted the living room.

6. I have been busy all week.

REPORTED SPEECH INTERVIEW

Work in groups of four or five. Choose one person to be interviewed. Ask him or her the eight questions below. Write down the answers in the blanks. Then take turns changing the answers to reported speech using the words *He said that . . .* or *She said that . . .*

Example: 1. Are you nervous?

   Answer: *No, I'm not nervous.*
   Reported Speech: He said that he wasn't nervous.

2. Are your eyes brown?

   _____.

3. Do you study a lot?

   _____.

4. Do you smoke?

   _____.

*Name*_____ *Date* _____

5. Did you eat breakfast today?

_____.

6. Did you read a newspaper?

_____.

7. Is it raining?

_____.

8. Have you visited Paris?

_____.

WRITING PRACTICE

Review the answers to the **Reported Speech Interview** above. Then write five of the answers in reported speech using the words *He said that* . . . or *She said that* . . .

1. _____.

2. _____.

3. _____.

4. _____.

5. _____.

READING PASSAGE

Many people are buying and repairing old buildings like those in Picture 10. Some people like old houses because they are cheap. Others want an unusual place to live. These buildings are very different from the thousands of small, square houses you see everywhere. Still others love old houses just because they are old.

Before you can repair a house like this, you have to clean it out. There may be old furniture and dishes inside. There is sure to be a lot of dirt. There are always broken windows to take care of. When the windows are repaired, wash down the walls and then the floors.

When the house is cleaned out, call in the electrician and plumber. First they will check the present systems. Then they will suggest changes. Tell them what you want, and they will tell you how much it will cost. Then they can begin work.

When these repairs are finished, the carpenter can begin. He will check floors, move walls, and put in new windows. Then he will finish the kitchen and bathroom. If you wish, he will even take care of painting the walls.

And now, if you have any money left, you can buy some furniture and move in.

READING QUESTIONS

Main Idea

Reread each paragraph and state its main idea in one sentence.

Paragraph One: *People like old houses for many reasons.*

Paragraph Two: _____.

Paragraph Three: _____.

Paragraph Four: _____.

WHEN DID IT HAPPEN?

Put a number one in front of the sentence that shows what happens first. Put a two in front of the second event, and so forth.

_____ You wash the floors.

_____ You take out the old furniture.

_____ You take care of broken windows.

_____ The carpenter will paint the walls.

_____ The carpenter will finish the bathroom.

_____ You wash down the walls.

_____ The carpenter will check the floors.

_____ The electrician will check your present system.

_____ The electrician will tell you the cost of changes.

_____ The electrician will suggest changes.

STRUCTURES

I	had	finished	breakfast
She	had	worked	for two days

when the phone	rang.
when she	quit.

	Original	*Reported Speech*
Ellen:	I'm busy.	She said that . . . she was busy. (past tense)
	I like my job. (present tense)	she liked her job. (past tense)
	I'm working hard. (present continuous tense)	she was working hard. (past continuous tense)
	I was late Monday. (past tense)	she had been late Monday. (past perfect tense)
	I worked late Friday. (past tense)	she had worked late Friday. (past perfect tense)
	I have been careful since then. (present perfect tense)	she had been careful since then. (past perfect tense)

Name _____ *Date* _____

VOCABULARY

Nouns	Verbs	Adjectives	Other
electrician	cost	original	behind
guest	return	square	finally
plumber	suggest	unusual	_____
price	_____	_____	_____
system	_____	_____	_____
thousands	_____	_____	_____
wood	_____	_____	_____
_____	_____	_____	_____

HOMEWORK

A. Be ready to complete each sentence using the present perfect tense.

   Example: 1. (to know)   Al _*haD known*_ for a year when they got married.

   2. (to wear)   He _____ that shirt only once when he washed it.

   3. (to sit)   Bill _____ there for 15 minutes when he fell asleep.

   4. (to park)   Ellen _____ the car when I came by.

   5. (to look at)   She _____ me for several minutes before she spoke.

   6. (to teach)   Mr. Wilson _____ for three years when he got his present job.

B. Write five sentences using present perfect tense followed by past tense. Use situations from your own life, if possible.

Name _____   Date _____

1. _____.

2. _____.

3. _____.

4. _____.

5. _____.

C. Be ready to change original speech into reported speech. Practice
    with the exercises on pages 84 and 85.

D. Change the following sentences to reported speech using the
    words *She said that* . . .

    1. I play tennis. _____.

    2. I finished early. _____.

    3. I'm sleepy. _____.

    4. I have seen that movie. _____.

    5. I was busy. _____.

    6. I wrote a letter to Jim. _____.

LISTENING EXERCISE

The teacher will read ten sentences. Change each one to reported
speech by filling in the missing words below.

1. The teacher said that _____ tired.

2. The teacher said that _____ here.

3. The teacher said that _____.

4. The teacher said that _____ at 8:00.

Name _____ *Date* _____

5. The teacher said that _____ early.

6. The teacher said that _____ a lot.

7. The teacher said that _____ the lesson.

8. The teacher said that _____ a new car.

9. The teacher said that _____ Karen.

10. The teacher said that _____ sure.

Unit 8

PICTURE TO TALK ABOUT

The man in Picture 12 plays baseball for the New York Yankees. Notice the use of *such* in the sentences below the picture. Repeat each sentence. Then say the sentences to another student. Later write in the missing words.

New York Yankees Photo

PICTURE 12

Name _____ Date _____

1. The Yankees are _____ _____ _____ _____ that they usually win.

2. Last year they had _____ _____ _____ that they couldn't believe it.

3. This man is _____ _____ _____ _____ that he gets a big salary.

4. He gets _____ _____ _____ _____ that he pays very high taxes.

5. He has _____ _____ _____ that he can run very fast.

6. Today there is _____ _____ _____ that he needs a cap.

7. The team takes _____ _____ _____ that sometimes he doesn't see his wife for weeks.

SUCH AND SUCH A

The sentences above use three patterns with *such* and *such a.* Sentences 1, 3, and 4 use Pattern One:

> *Such + A + Adjective + Singular Noun*
> such a good   team

Sentences 5 and 7 use Pattern Two:

> *Such + Adjective + Plural Noun*
> such long legs

Sentences 2 and 6 use Pattern Three:

> *Such + Adjective + Uncountable Noun*
> such good   luck

See *Adult English One,* Unit 7, for an introduction to countable and uncountable nouns.

Name _____ *Date* _____

Sentences with *such* and *such a* can also be written with *so*. See *Adult English Two,* Unit 6, for the pattern *So + Adjective + That.* Using the *so* pattern, the above sentences would be:

1. The Yankees are *so good that* they usually win.

5. His legs are *so long that* he can run very fast.

2. Their luck was *so good that* they couldn't believe it.

PRACTICE *SUCH* AND *SUCH A*

Work in pairs. Take turns combining the pairs of sentences using *such* and *such a.* Use Patterns One, Two, and Three.

Example: 1. That table is heavy. I can't pick it up.

That is *such a heavy table* that I can't pick it up.

2. Mr. Miller is a careful driver. He never has accidents.

3. Mr. Miller tells wonderful stories. I could listen for hours.

4. Al is very talkative. He makes me nervous.

5. This coffee is very hot. I can't drink it.

6. Ellen has noisy neighbors. She can't sleep at night.

7. The weather was very cold. I didn't leave the house.

8. Bill is very serious. He never laughs.

Name _____ Date _____

MORE *SUCH/SUCH A* PRACTICE

Work in groups of four or five. Take turns making *such/such a* sentences using the cue words below.

Example: 1. cold day — couldn't swim.

It was *such a cold day* that we couldn't swim.

2. young children — couldn't go to school

3. good food — ate a lot

4. sunny day — went swimming

5. difficult problems — couldn't do them

6. hard work — got tired fast

7. dirty restaurant — didnt eat there

8. smart student — got 100 on her exam

SO AND *SUCH A*

Work in pairs. First read the sentences below. Be sure that you understand each one. Then take turns saying each sentence using *such* or *such a* instead of *so*.

Example: 1. Billy was so lazy that he slept until noon.

Billy was such a lazy boy that he slept until noon.

Name _____ *Date* _____

2. That car is so expensive that I can't buy it.

3. Those players are so good that they usually win.

4. Her kitchen is so clean that you can eat off the floor.

5. The weather was so rainy that we stayed home.

6. The man was so strange that I ran away.

7. They are so friendly that I visit them often.

8. The tea was so good that I had three cups.

WRITING PRACTICE

Review the **More *Such/Such a* Practice** section. Then write five of the sentences below using *such* or *such a*.

1. _____.

2. _____.

3. _____.

4. _____.

5. _____.

TALK ABOUT CHART 1

Look at Chart 1. It describes the lives of four people. Notice the use of *so* and *neither* in the sentences in the following chart. Repeat each sentence. Then say the sentences to another student. Later write in the missing words.

Name _____ Date _____

95

CHART 1

	is	studied	has played	is living in	likes
Howard	quiet	farming	(only) baseball	a house	hot weather
Ken	quiet	farming	baseball and soccer	a single room	cold weather
Beverly	talkative	business	(only) tennis	an apartment	cold weather
Bill	talkative	business	(only) baseball	an apartment	hot weather

1. Howard is quiet _____ _____ _____ Ken.

2. Beverly isn't quiet _____ _____ _____ Bill.

3. Howard studied farming _____ _____ _____ Ken.

4. Beverly didn't study farming _____ _____ _____ Bill.

5. Howard has played baseball _____ _____ _____ Bill.

6. Beverly hasn't played soccer _____ _____ _____ Howard.

SO AND *NEITHER*

Sentences 1, 3, and 5 use the pattern:

And + *So* + Affirmative Helping Verb + Person

(Present tense)	and	so	is	Ken
(Past tense)	and	so	did	Ken
(Present perfect tense)	and	so	has	Bill

The helping verb in the *so/neither* part is always the same tense as the main verb. The above pattern is used when the main verb is affirmative.

The following pattern is used when the main verb is negative. See sentences 2, 4, and 6.

And + *Neither* + Negative Helping Verb + Person

(Present tense) and	neither	is	Bill
(Past tense) and	neither	did	Bill
(Present perfect tense) and	neither	has	Howard

Sentences with *so* and *neither* can also be written with *too* and *either*. See *Adult English One,* Unit 10, for the patterns:

And + Person + Affirmative Helping Verb + Too

and

And + Person + Negative Helping Verb + Either

Using the *too/either* patterns, sentences 1 and 2 would be:

Howard is quiet, *and Ken is too.*

Beverly isn't quiet, *and Bill isn't either.*

PRACTICE *SO* AND *NEITHER*

Work in pairs. Take turns completing the sentences using information from Chart 1. Be sure that the helping verb you choose is the same tense as the main verb.

Example: 1. Howard didn't study business . . .

Howard didn't study business and neither did Ken.

2. Howard hasn't played tennis . . .

3. Howard isn't living in an apartment . . .

4. Beverly is living in an apartment . . .

5. Howard likes hot weather . . .

6. Ken doesn't like hot weather . . .

Name _____ Date _____

7. Beverly isn't living in a house . . .

8. Ken likes cold weather . . .

MORE *SO/NEITHER* PRACTICE

Work in groups of four or five. Take turns combining the pairs of sentences below using *so* and *neither*.

Example: 1. I am waiting. They are waiting.

           I am waiting *and so are they*.

2. We sing well. Beverly sings well.

3. Bill graduated last year. Howard graduated last year.

4. Howard has gone to bed. Ken has gone to bed.

5. I saw Ellen last week. Bill saw Ellen last week.

6. I'm tired. You're tired.

7. Al was late to work. We were late to work.

8. Beverly has finished high school. I have finished high school.

SO/NEITHER AND *TOO/EITHER*

Work in pairs. First read the sentences below. Be sure that you understand each one. Then take turns saying each sentence using *so* or *neither* instead of *too* or *either*.

Example: 1. I don't like math and Bill doesn't either.

           I don't like math and neither does Bill.

2. I left early and Ellen did too.

3. Howard didn't visit Paris and I didn't either.

Name _____ Date _____

Unit 9

PICTURE TO TALK ABOUT

George's life is a sad story. He left home when he was fourteen. Now, at thirty-five, he is a bum. He has no home and no friends. The teacher will describe what has happened to George. Repeat each sentence. Then say the sentences to another student. Later write in the missing words.

Paul Knipping, Dewys, Inc.

PICTURE 13

Name _____ Date _____

1. George left home at fourteen. He didn't finish school.

    If he _____ _____ home, he _____ _____ _____ school.

2. He started drinking. He couldn't get a job.

    If he _____ _____ drinking, he _____ _____ _____ a job.

3. He had no money. He couldn't rent a room.

    If he _____ _____ money, he _____ _____ _____ a room.

4. He wanted to ask his family for help, but he was ashamed.

    He _____ _____ _____ his family for help if he _____

    _____ ashamed.

5. His family _____ _____ _____ him if he _____ _____ them.

6. He got sick and almost died. A policeman took him to a hospital.

    He _____ _____ _____ if a policeman _____ _____ him

    to a hospital.

UNREAL PAST CONDITIONAL

(For real present conditional see *Adult English One*, Unit 14. For unreal present conditional see *Adult English Two*, Unit 13.)

The unreal past conditional is used to describe events that did *not* happen. The *if* clause tells about a condition that was not present. The main clause describes a result that did not happen. The whole sentence expresses an idea about how things might have been different in the past, if conditions had been different at that time.

Name _____ *Date* _____

The *if* clause uses the Past Perfect Tense. The main clause uses *would* + Present Perfect Tense, *could* + Present Perfect Tense, or *might* + Present Perfect Tense. The sentence can begin with either the main clause or the *if* clause.

Example 1:   (See sentence 5.)

His family *would have helped* him if he *had asked* them.

Would + Present	Past
Perfect	Perfect
Tense	Tense

The *would* shows that the result was sure to happen at that time.

Example 2:   (See sentence 2.)

If he *hadn't started* drinking, he *could have gotten* a job.

Past	*Could* + Present
Perfect	Perfect
Tense	Tense

The *could* shows that the result was possible at that time.

Example 3:   (See sentence 1.)

If he *hadn't left* home, he *might have finished* school.

Past	*Might* + Past
Perfect	Perfect
Tense	Tense

The *might* shows that the result was possible at that time, but not as definite as with *could*.

ORAL PRACTICE

Work in pairs. Take turns making unreal past conditionals by combining an *if* clause from Column A with a main clause from Column B.

Example: 1. If I had stayed home, I could have slept all day.

Column A	Column B
1. I had stayed home	*Would*
2. you had stayed longer	have been tired
3. you had finished school	not have bought it
4. she had tried on the coat	*Could*
5. he had explained the problem	have gotten a better job
6. I had worked hard	have had breakfast at home
7. I had studied more	have slept all day
8. I had gotten up earlier	*Might*
	have met Alice
	have passed the test
	have understood

Now say these sentences with the *if* clause last. Practice the sentences with another student.

Example: I could have slept all day if I had stayed home.

COMPLETION EXERCISE

Work in groups of three or four. Take turns completing the sentences using a clause with *would, could,* or *might* + Present Perfect Tense. Try to complete each sentence two or three different ways.

Example: 1. If I had walked to school, *I would have been late.*

I might have seen you.

Name _____   Date _____

2. If I had stayed home yesterday,

3. If I had learned English ten years ago,

4. If I had gotten up early Sunday,

5. If he had locked the door,

6. If she had cooked dinner,

7. If he had cleaned the house,

8. If she had put her money in the bank,

MORE PRACTICE WITH UNREAL PAST CONDITIONAL

Work in pairs. Read the sentences below. Then take turns paraphrasing each pair of sentences using the unreal past conditional.

Example: 1. Grace got up late. She didn't have breakfast.

If Grade hadn't gotten up late, she would have had breakfast.

2. She didn't drive to school. She was late.

3. She wasn't early. She didn't have time for coffee.

4. Grace was late. She couldn't help Marie with her homework.

5. Grace was worried about something. She didn't listen to the lesson.

6. She didn't listen to the lesson. She didn't understand it.

7. She didn't understand the lesson. She didn't pass the test.

8. She didn't pass the test. She wasn't happy.

Name _____ Date _____

WRITING PRACTICE

Review the **Oral Practice** section. Then write five of the sentences below.

1. _____.

2. _____.

3. _____.

4. _____.

5. _____.

TALK ABOUT WEIGHTS AND MEASURES

Go over the vocabulary used in Picture 14. Be sure you understand each measure of weight and distance. Repeat each sentence after the teacher. Then say the sentences to another student. Later write in the missing words.

PICTURE 14

Name _____ Date _____

1. There are _____ ounces in a pound.

2. There are _____ grams in a kilogram.

3. An ounce is about _____ grams.

4. A pound is about _____ grams.

5. There are _____ inches in a foot.

6. There are _____ feet in a yard.

7. There are _____ centimeters in a meter.

8. An inch is about _____ centimeters.

9. A foot is about _____ centimeters.

10. A yard is about _____ centimeters.

ORAL PRACTICE

Work in pairs. Take turns filling in the blanks in the sentences below. Have the teacher check your answers.

Distance

1. I am about _____ feet tall. I am about _____ centimeters tall.

2. This desk is about _____ feet high. It's about _____ centimeters high.

Name_____ Date _____

3. This book is about _____ inches long. It's about _____ centimeters long.

4. This book is about _____ inches wide. It's about _____ centimeters wide.

5. This room is about _____ yards long. It's about _____ meters long.

Weight

1. I weigh about _____ pounds. I weigh about _____ kilograms.

2. The desk weighs about _____ pounds. It weighs about _____ kilograms.

3. My pencil weighs about _____ ounces. It weighs about _____ grams.

4. An egg weighs about _____ ounces. An egg weighs about _____ grams.

5. A car weighs about _____ pounds. A car weighs about _____ kilograms.

GROUP PRACTICE

Work in groups of three or four. The first person writes a weight on a piece of paper using abbreviations. He or she holds up the paper so all group members can see it. The second person reads the weight out loud. The third person makes a sentence using that weight.

Example: First Person: holds up a piece of paper saying *10 lbs.*

Second Person: says *ten pounds.*

Third Person: says *That desk weighs ten pounds.*

Repeat the exercise several times. Practice using all the measures of weight and distance.

WRITING PRACTICE

Write sentences using the cue words below. Write out all abbreviations.

Example: 1. book   1 lb.

_The book weighs one pound_____.

2. window   2 M.   wide

_____.

3. my wallet   6 oz.

_____.

4. the door   1 yd.   wide

_____.

5. the letter   30 gm.

_____.

6. my brother   6 ft.   tall

_____.

7. my hand   3 in.   wide

_____.

8. a bicycle   3 ft.   tall

_____.

READING PASSAGE

George did not have a happy childhood. He was one of seven children in a very poor family. Often he didn't have enough to eat. Sometimes his father got angry and hit him. His clothes were so old that the other school children laughed at him.

George tried hard to make a good life for himself. He studied a lot, but school was difficult for him. When he was thirteen he tried to find a part-time job, but he couldn't get one. At fourteen he left home hoping to find a better life somewhere else.

But George's life got worse instead of better. He began to drink a lot. Soon he had no money and no place to sleep. Then he got very sick and almost died. If a policeman hadn't taken him to a hospital, he might have died.

The trip to the hospital was lucky for George in other ways. He met a social worker named Gil Benson. Gil helped him find a place to stay after he left the hospital. Then he helped George find a job in a restaurant. Now he has a steady job. George is not completely happy. There are many things in his life that he wants to change. But he is making a better life for himself.

Name _____ Date _____

Finding Details

In Units 5 and 6 you picked out the main idea of each paragraph of the reading passage. In Units 7 and 8 you reread each paragraph and stated its main idea in a sentence. This time you are given the main idea of each paragraph. Your job is to find two details that support each main idea. Then copy these details in the blanks below each main idea.

Example: Paragraph One

George had an unhappy childhood.

He didn't have enough to eat.

His father hit him

Paragraph Two

George tried to make a good life for himself.

_____.

_____.

Paragraph Three

George's life got worse after he left home.

_____.

_____.

Paragraph Four

The trip to the hospital was lucky for George.

_____.

_____.

Name _____ *Date* _____

WHEN DID IT HAPPEN?

Put a number one in front of the sentence that shows what happened first. Put a two in front of the second event, and so forth.

_____ George got sick and almost died.

_____ George studied hard.

_____ George met a social worker.

_____ George couldn't get a job.

_____ Gil helped George find a place to stay.

_____ George left home.

_____ George got a job in a restaurant.

_____ George began to drink a lot.

_____ George had no place to sleep.

_____ George is making a better life for himself.

STRUCTURES

Past
Perfect
Tense

If he	had asked	them,
If he	hadn't started	drinking,
If he	hadn't left	home,

Would
Could + Present Perfect Tense
Might

his family	would	have helped	him.
he	could	have gotten	a job.
he	might	have finished	school.

Name _____ Date _____

116

VOCABULARY

Nouns	Verbs	Adjectives
abbreviation	weigh	ashamed
bum	_____	high
childhood	_____	steady
distance	_____	wide
social worker	_____	_____
test	_____	_____
weight	_____	_____
_____	_____	_____
_____	_____	_____

Other (Weights and Distances)

Measure	Abbreviation
centimeter	cm.
foot	ft.
gram	gm.
inch	in.
kilogram	kg.
meter	M.
ounce	oz.
pound	lb.
yard.	yd.

HOMEWORK

A. Review the **Oral Practice** section on page 106. Be ready to say any of the eight sentences during the next class.

Name _____ Date _____

B. Review the **More Practice with Unreal Past Conditional** section. Then write five of the sentences below.

1. _____.

2. _____.

3. _____.

4. _____.

5. _____.

C. Memorize the ten fill-ins under Picture 14. Be ready to say all ten sentences during the next class.

D. Figure out how much the following objects weigh and how long they are: your shoe, a banana, a telephone, a knife, a horse, a sofa.

LISTENING EXERCISE

Fill in the missing words.

1. It weighs _____ _____.

2. The room is _____ _____ long.

3. She's _____ _____ tall.

4. That chair weighs _____ _____.

5. The door is _____ _____ wide.

6. Give me _____ _____ of chocolate.

7. This pencil is _____ _____ long.

8. That book weighs about _____ _____.

9. _____ _____ is one meter.

10. One ounce is about _____ _____.

Name _____ *Date* _____

Unit 10

PICTURE TO TALK ABOUT

Lenny works on an automobile assembly line in Detroit. He is a very independent man. Repeat each sentence below. Be sure that you understand the meaning of each one. Then say the sentences to another student. Later write in the missing words.

General Motors Corporation

PICTURE 15

Name _____ Date _____

1. Lenny always works _____ _____.

2. No one checks Lenny's work. He checks it _____.

3. Sometimes Lenny talks _____ _____.

4. Lenny lives _____ _____.

5. No one cooks or sews for him. He does these things _____.

6. He is proud _____ _____.

REFLEXIVE PRONOUNS

This unit introduces three reflexive pronoun patterns.

Pattern 1:   (See sentences 1 and 4 above.)

By + Reflexive Pronoun

Lenny always works *by himself.*

Lenny lives *by himself.*

By + Reflexive Pronoun means *alone.* You can paraphrase the sentences above this way: Lenny always works alone. Lenny lives alone.

Pattern 2:   (see sentences 3 and 6 above.)

Prepositions
Except *By* + Reflexive Pronoun

Sometimes he talks *to himself.*

He is proud *of himself.*

Preposition + Reflexive Pronoun is used instead of repeating the subject of the sentence.

Wrong: Lenny talks to Lenny.
Wrong: Lenny talks to him. (This means Lenny talks to another person.)
Right: Lenny talks to himself.

Pattern 3:   (See sentences 2 and 5 above.)

Reflexive
Pronoun

He checks it *himself.*

He does these things *himself.*

Sometimes there is no preposition before the reflexive pronoun. Then the reflexive pronoun emphasizes that the subject of the sentence did the action, when you might expect another person to do it. You might expect someone else to check his work or do his cooking and sewing.

There are eight reflexive pronouns. Fill in the missing ones.

```
 _____        _____


 _____        _____


 _____


 _____        _____


 _____
```

PRACTICE REFLEXIVE PRONOUNS

Work in pairs. Take turns making sentences with reflexive pronouns by combining an item from Column A with one from Column B.

Name _____ *Date* _____

Example: 1. We are happy with ourselves.

Column A	Column B
1. We are happy	Pattern 1:
2. I like to study	by himself
3. The baby can walk	by myself
4. Sometimes you talk	by itself
5. We repaired the car	Pattern 2:
6. They are proud	to yourself
7. He lives	of themselves
8. You can paint the room	with ourselves
	Pattern 3:
	ourselves
	yourselves

MORE PRACTICE WITH REFLEXIVE PRONOUNS

Work in groups of four or five. Take turns paraphrasing the sentences below.

Example: 1. George is worried about his health.

George is worried about himself.

2. I repaired the watch. (I didn't go to a jeweler.)

3. Alice flew the plane. (The pilot didn't fly it.)

4. Rita is proud of her new clothes.

5. Billy went to the store alone.

6. Ellen likes to take long walks alone.

7. Those people are happy with their lives.

8. Marie changed the flat tire. (Her husband didn't change it.)

9. My grandfather lives alone.

10. Mr. Wilson cooked dinner. (His wife didn't do it.)

QUESTIONS AND ANSWERS

Work in pairs. Take turns answering the questions below using the three reflexive pronoun patterns.

Example: 1. Do you live alone?

No, I don't live by myself.

2. Do you ever talk to yourself?

3. Did you do the washing, or did your mother do it?

4. Do you like to study with a lot of other people around?

5. Do your friends ever write notes to themselves?

6. Do you ever go to a movie alone?

7. Did you do your homework, or did you copy someone else's work?

8. Do you ever worry about your future?

WRITING PRACTICE

Review the **Questions and Answers** section. Then write five of the answers on the following page.

Name _____ *Date* _____

1. _____.

2. _____.

3. _____.

4. _____.

5. _____.

PICTURE TO TALK ABOUT

The Davidson family took a long trip by bus last summer. One of the places they visited was Washington, D.C. The teacher will tell about the trip. Be sure you understand the meaning of each sentence. Then repeat each one. After that say the sentences to another student. Later write in the missing words.

The Greyhound Corporation

PICTURE 16

-ed Adjectives

1. The day they left home, the children were _____.

2. They were _____ how big the bus was.

Name _____ *Date* _____

3. They were _____ in the other passengers.

4. After six hours of riding, Mr. Davidson was very _____.

5. Mrs. Davidson was _____.

-ing Adjectives

1. The trip was _____ for the whole family.

2. They had many _____ experiences.

3. Washington was the most _____ city.

4. The trip was _____. It lasted 21 days.

5. Some places they visited were _____.

-ed and -ing Adjectives

The -ed and -ing words in the sentences above are adjectives.

The -ed words describe _____.

The -ing words describe _____.

PRACTICE -ED AND -ING ADJECTIVES

Work in groups of four or five. Take turns filling in the blanks in each pair of sentences. Use the word in parentheses to make one -ed and one -ing adjective.

Example: 1. (bore)   The class was _____. (class = thing)

The students felt _____. (students = people)

2. (surprise)   The child gave a _____ answer.

Its parents were _____.

3. (confuse)   I am _____ by this map.

This map is _____.

4. (interest)   The old cars are _____.

I am _____ in old cars.

5. (tire)   I am really _____.

Baseball is really _____.

6. (disappoint)   The food was terrible. It was a _____ meal.

We were very _____.

QUESTIONS AND ANSWERS

Work in pairs. Take turns answering the questions using *-ed* and *-ing* adjectives.

Example: 1. Do you like to study math?   (interest, bore)

Yes, math is *interesting*.

No, I am *bored* when I study math.

2. How do you feel about fishing?   (interest, bore)

3. How do you feel after running for 15 minutes?   (tire)

4. Is English always easy and clear?   (confuse)

5. How do you feel when it rains on your picnic?   (disappoint)

6. Do you like clowns?   (amuse)

Name _____ Date _____

MORE *-ED* AND *-ING* PRACTICE

Work in pairs. Take turns using the following words to make *-ed* and *-ing* fill-ins for the sentences below.

amuse	confuse	excite	surprise
bore	disappoint	interest	tire

1. I went to bed because I was _____.

2. I am _____ with serious music.

3. Baby animals are often funny. Some are really _____.

4. I am _____ about my new car.

5. French is an _____ language.

6. Ellen got a sofa for her birthday. That's a _____ present!

7. Getting a bad mark on a test is _____.

8. Cleaning the house is _____ work.

9. I get _____ in strange cities.

10. When Mr. Wilson put on a dress, everyone was _____.

WRITING PRACTICE

Review the **Questions and Answers** section. Then write five of the answers below.

1. _____.

2. _____.

3. _____.

4. _____.

5. _____.

READING PASSAGE

The Davidsons took a three-week bus trip last summer. The children were excited for weeks before they left. The Davidsons traveled more than 3,000 miles and passed through twelve different states. The children counted the number of cities they spent time in. The total was twenty four!

Each day was full of interesting events. In the first city they visited several museums. In the next city they went to the tops of all the tall buildings. Then they toured a factory and saw how furniture is made. Later on they visited a farm and saw how vegetables are grown. Near the end of the trip they spent a day swimming in the ocean. They didn't have a single boring day!

But the Davidsons were very happy to return home. Billy ran next door to show Jim the postcards he had bought. A few minutes later Marie called up her girlfriend, Susan, and they talked on the phone for an hour. Mrs. Davidson went food shopping. Then she sat down happily in front of the television and didn't move for hours. Mr. Davidson sat down in his favorite chair and read the newspaper. They were all very tired that night. The trip had been wonderful, but being home was wonderful, too.

READING QUESTIONS

Finding Details

You are given the main idea of each paragraph in the reading passage. Find two details that support each main idea. Then write the details in the blanks below each main idea.

Paragraph One: The Davidsons visited many different places.

_____.

_____.

Paragraph Two: Each day of the trip was interesting.

_____.

_____.

Paragraph Three: They were happy to get home.

_____.

_____.

WHEN DID IT HAPPEN?

Put a number one in front of the sentence that shows what happened first. Put a two in front of the second event, and so forth.

_____   They saw how furniture was made.

_____   They visited a farm.

_____   They were all tired that night.

_____   They spent a day swimming in the ocean.

_____   The children were excited for weeks before the trip.

_____   They visited several museums.

_____   Mrs. Davidson watched television for hours.

_____   They went to the tops of several tall buildings.

_____   Marie called up her girlfriend.

_____   Billy showed his postcards to Jim.

Name _____   Date _____

STRUCTURES

I live	by	myself.
Sometimes he talks	to	himself.
They are proud	of	themselves.
She repairs the car		herself.

(*By* + Reflexive Pronoun)

(*To*
(*Of* + Reflexive Pronoun)
(*With*

(Reflexive Pronoun Only)

The movie is	interesting.	
I am	interested	in the movie.

VOCABULARY

Nouns	Verbs	Adjectives	Other
assembly line	count	favorite	_____
clown	sew	independent	_____
experiences	_____	_____	_____
map	_____	_____	_____
meal	_____	_____	_____
museum	_____	_____	_____
note	_____	_____	_____
picnic	_____	_____	_____
postcard	_____	_____	_____
tire	_____	_____	_____
total	_____	_____	_____
washing	_____	_____	_____
_____	_____	_____	_____

Name _____ Date _____

HOMEWORK

A. Make up six sentences about yourself using reflexive pronouns. Be ready to say two sentences for Pattern 1, two sentences for Pattern 2, and two sentences for Pattern 3.

B. Review the **More Practice with Reflexive Pronouns** section. Then write five or the sentences below.

1. _____.

2. _____.

3. _____.

4. _____.

5. _____.

C. Use the list of words below to make up sentences about your life. Make three sentences with *-ed* adjectives and three sentences with *-ing* adjectives. Be ready to say these sentences during the next class.

    bore   confuse   excite   interest   surprise   tire

D. There are four sentences in the reading passage that contain *-ed* and *-ing* adjectives. Locate the four sentences and copy them below.

1. _____.

2. _____.

3. _____.

4. _____.

LISTENING EXERCISE

Fill in the missing words.

1. I went for a walk _____ _____.

Name _____ *Date* _____

2. When I saw that movie I was _____.

3. It was an _____ movie.

4. They are proud _____ _____.

5. The book was _____.

6. I was _____ by that book.

7. She painted that table _____.

8. Playing tennis is _____.

9. A cat can wash _____.

10. He cooked dinner _____.

Unit 11

PICTURE TO TALK ABOUT

Ruth and Dan Nolan bought a camper last spring. They traveled for four weeks last summer. The teacher will describe their experiences using *-ing* words. Repeat each sentence. Then say the sentences to another student. Later write in the missing words.

Fleetwood Enterprises Incorporated

PICTURE 17

Name _____ Date _____

1. Both the Nolans enjoy _____.

2. Dan suggested _____ a camper to use on vacation.

3. They tried _____ a van, and soon bought one.

4. The Nolans were proud of _____ a new camper. They had a wonderful trip.

5. Each morning they were happy about _____ up early.

6. They finished _____ breakfast by 8:00.

7. Dan usually started _____.

8. When he was tired of _____, Ruth took over.

9. They liked _____ their home with them.

10. They were never worried about _____ a place to sleep.

-*ING* WORDS

The sentences above contain -*ing* words used in three patterns. Sentences 1 and 7 use pattern one:

Verb + -*ing* Word

The Nolans *enjoy   driving*.

Sentences 2, 3, 6, and 9 used pattern two:

Verb + *ing* Word

Dan *suggested   buying* a camper.

Sentences 4, 5, 8, and 10 use pattern three:

Adjective + Preposition + *ing* Word

The Nolans were *proud   of   having* a new camper.

Not all verbs can be used before an *-ing* word. Chart 1 lists verbs that can be used.

CHART 1

*begin	remember
*continue	*start
enjoy	stop
finish	suggest
*like	*try
practice	

*Verbs marked with a * can be used in the patterns Verb + Infinitive (I like to eat.) and Verb + Infinitive + Noun (He likes to play tennis.). The other verbs can *not* be used in Verb + Infinitive patterns. (See *Adult English Two*, Unit 5 for Verb + Infinitive pattern.)

PRACTICING USING *-ING* WORDS

Work in pairs. Take turns making sentences with *-ing* words by combining an item from Column A with one from Column B. Add extra words as necessary.

Example: 1. I enjoy swimming.

Column A	*Column B*
1. enjoy	walking
2. likes	smoking
3. are afraid of	swimming
4. suggested	doing his homework
5. remembered	locking the door
6. is excited about	watching television
7. stopped	failing the exam
8. finished	winning $5,000

Name _____ Date _____

QUESTIONS AND ANSWERS

Work in groups of four or five. Take turns asking and answering the questions below using the verbs in parentheses. Answer each question using the verb in parentheses plus an *-ing* word.

Example: 1. Do you smoke any more?   (stop)

No, I stopped smoking.

2. When did you begin to study English?   (start)

3. Did Dan have breakfast at 9:00?   (finish)

4. Do you like to play soccer?   (enjoy)

5. Do you speak English after class?   (practice)

6. Did you see Luis last week?   (remember)

7. What idea did Dan have?   (suggest)

8. What do you like to do Saturday mornings?   (enjoy)

MORE QUESTIONS AND ANSWERS

Work in pairs. Take turns asking and answering questions using the cue words below. Use an *-ing* pattern in all questions and answers.

Example: 1. Did you begin working last year?

Yes, I began working last year.

1. begin   work   last year

2. enjoy   sleep   ten hours a night

3. bored with   do   homework

4. remember   lock   your door

5. continue   study English   next year

Name _____ Date _____

6. good at   take care of   children

7. like   cook   dinner

8. afraid of   get   sick

WRITING PRACTICE

All of the sentences below have Verb + Infinitive. Four of the sentences are wrong because the verbs can *not* be followed by an infinitive. Copy the four correct sentences keeping the Verb + Infinitive pattern. Change the four incorrect sentences to the Verb + *ing* Word pattern. (See Chart 1 to find out which verbs cannot be followed by an infinitive.)

1. He tried to ride the bicycle.

   _____.

2. Did they suggest to visit Al?

   _____?

3. They started to leave early.

   _____.

4. I like to swim in the ocean.

   _____.

5. They practice to repair the car.

   _____.

6. Did you finish to eat your lunch yet?

   _____?

7. Should I continue to take the medicine?

   _____?

8. We always enjoy to see her.

   _____.

READING PASSAGE

Their new camper helps make traveling easy for the Nolans. They don't have to carry luggage in and out of hotels. They never have to get dressed up for dinner. They don't have to worry about finding a place to spend the night. They can stop and take a nap whenever they want to. The Nolans wonder why everyone doesn't travel by camper.

The Nolans save money using a camper. They never pay hotel or motel bills. They cook all their own meals in the camper. Sometimes they even wash and dry clothes overnight. They do have to pay for gas. But if they drove a car, they would have to pay for gas anyway.

There were some problems. It was no fun to drive a camper in a strong wind. Sometimes campsites were full when they arrived. Once the refrigerator stopped working and they lost all of their food. But all in all the Nolans enjoy having their camper.

READING QUESTIONS

Main Idea

Reread each paragraph and state its main idea in one sentence.

Paragraph One: _____.

Paragraph Two: _____.

Paragraph Three: _____.

VOCABULARY PRACTICE

Fill in the blanks using the following eight words:

afraid   camper   dressed up   refrigerator

all in all   campsite   early   trip

1. We arrived _____ in the morning.

2. The Nolans cook in their _____.

3. They took a long _____.

4. They weren't _____ of having an accident.

5. They never get _____ for dinner.

6. A _____ keeps food cold.

7. _____ it was a good trip.

8. They park their camper in a _____ every night.

STRUCTURES

-ing Word

Bill	enjoys	eating.		(Pattern 1)
Bill	enjoys	playing.	football.	(Pattern 2)
Bill	is excited about	flying	to California.	(Pattern 3)

VOCABULARY

Nouns	Verbs	Adjectives	Other
camper	_____	afraid	all in all
campsite	_____	dressed up	overnight
refrigerator	_____	early	_____
trip	_____	_____	_____
_____	_____	_____	_____
_____	_____	_____	_____

HOMEWORK

A. Memorize Chart 1. Be ready to pick out sentences in which the pattern Verb + Infinitive cannot be used.

B. Review **Practicing Using -*ing* Words.** Be ready to say eight sentences combining items from Column A and Column B.

C. Review the **Questions and Answers** section. Then write three sets of questions and answers on a separate sheet of paper.

D. Write five sentences using the pattern Adjective + Preposition + -*ing* Word. Use the items in parentheses to make your sentences.

    1. (proud of) _____.

    2. (good at) _____.

    3. (tired of) _____.

    4. (sure about) _____.

    5. (bored with) _____.

Name _____ Date _____

LISTENING PRACTICE

Fill in the missing words.

1. Are you _____ _____ your sister?

2. When did she _____ _____ ?

3. I'm _____ _____ you.

4. Have you _____ _____ that book yet?

5. The teacher _____ _____ a dictionary.

6. I'm _____ _____ my mark on the test.

7. Do you _____ _____ in the city?

8. She _____ _____ last year.

9. I'm _____ _____ working.

10. I _____ _____ the book yesterday.

Name _____ Date _____

Unit 12

PICTURE TO TALK ABOUT

Mr. Williams and his students went to an amusement park. They took a ride on the roller coaster. Wanda sat next to Mr. Williams. She was very frightened. The teacher will describe their feelings using the word *wish*. Repeat each sentence. Then say the sentences to another student. Later write in the missing words.

Great Adventure

PICTURE 18

Name _____ Date _____

Present

1. Wanda wishes that she _____ on the ground right now.

2. She wishes that the roller coaster _____ slower.

3. Mr. Williams wishes that he _____ safer.

Past

4. Wanda wishes that she _____ _____ home.

5. Mr. Williams wishes that he _____ _____ the children here.

6. The children wish that they _____ _____ on the roller coaster.

Future

7. Wanda wishes that the ride _____ _____ soon.

8. The children wish that Mr. Williams _____ _____ the roller coaster stop.

9. Mr. Williams wishes that Wanda _____ _____ a little.

WISH CLAUSES

Wishing About Present Situations

Sentences 1, 2, and 3 are examples of uncomfortable present situations. The people would like these situations to be different. Wishes about present situations use Past Tense verbs.

Pattern 1:	*Wish*	+ *That*	+ Subject		+ *Past* Tense	
Wanda	*wishes*	*that*	*she*		*were*	on the ground.
She	*wishes*	*that*	*the roller coaster*		*were going* slower.	

Wishing About Past Situations

Sentences 4, 5, and 6 are examples of things that people should have done differently in the past. These people feel that they have made mistakes. Wishes about past situations use Past Perfect Tense Verbs. (See *Adult English Three,* Unit 7, for a review of the Past Perfect Tense.)

Pattern 2:	*Wish*	+ *That*	+ Subject	+ Past Perfect Tense	
Wanda	*wishes*	*that*	*she*	*had stayed*	home.
Mr. Williams	*wishes*	*that*	*he*	*hadn't brought*	them here.

Wishing About Future Situations

Sentences 7, 8, and 9 are examples of things that people want to have happen in the future. Wishes about the future use *Would* + Base Form.

Pattern 3:	*Wish*	+ *That*	+ Subject	+ *Would*	+ Base Form	
Wanda	*wishes*	*that*	*the ride*	*would*	*stop*	soon.
Mr. Williams	*wishes*	*that*	*Wanda*	*would*	*relax.*	

PRACTICE WISHING

Work in pairs. Take turns using the three patterns to make sentences about the situations below.

Example: 1. I wish *that the weather were warm.*

---

*In written wish clauses the past tense of *to be* is always *were.* In spoken English you may use *was* or *were* with the third person singular.

Name _____ Date _____

1. The weather isn't warm.

2. I don't speak French.

3. I don't have a car.

Past Situations

4. I didn't have breakfast today.

5. I didn't see you yesterday.

6. Dan didn't finish the book.

Future Situations

7. It didn't stop raining yet.

8. The teacher didn't come yet.

9. I didn't get a letter this week.

MORE WISHES

Work in pairs. This time one person reads a statement below, and the other person responds with a *wish* sentence. There may be more than one correct response to each statement.

Example: 1. I wish that I *were warm.*   (Present situation)

       I wish that I *had worn* a coat.   (Past situation)

       I wish that you *would give* me your coat.   (Future situation)

2. I'm cold.

3. I'm late to work.

4. Ruth doesn't have a job. She is trying to get one.

Name _____ Date _____

5. Grandfather isn't happy about being old.

6. Dan forgot his umbrella.

7. I'm waiting for my friend to get here.

A STORY FULL OF PROBLEMS

Work in groups of four or five. Read the story together. Be sure that you understand each line. Then take turns making *wish* sentences about Wanda. Use all three patterns.

Wanda is taking a math test. She's nervous. She's tired, too.

She didn't listen in class. She didn't read the math book. She didn't do the homework either. She played outside last night. She didn't study for the test.

She wants the teacher to help her with the test, but he won't. She wants the test to end soon.

Example: Wanda wishes that she *weren't taking* a math test.

WRITING PRACTICE

Write five of the wish sentences from the story above.

1. _____.

2. _____.

3. _____.

4. _____.

5. _____.

READING PASSAGE

Mr. Williams thinks that children learn from books, but he uses many other ways of teaching. He shows movies. He invites community people to speak to the students. This year a policeman and a nurse have visited the class. The students keep animals like frogs and mice at school. They grow vegetables in a box near the window.

The children work very hard. They always do their homework. They help Mr. Williams keep the room clean. They take care of the plants and animals all by themselves. Often they stay after school for extra help.

The children's parents like Mr. Williams. They sent a letter to the principal telling what a good job he was doing. Every week one of the mothers spends a half day helping him with the class. At the end of the year the parents gave him a party. Not many teachers are as well liked as Mr. Williams.

READING QUESTIONS

Write T in front of true sentences and F in front of false ones.

Fact

_____ 1. Mr. Williams thinks students learn from books.

_____ 2. The children don't work hard.

_____ 3. The children sometimes stay after school.

_____ 4. The children keep the room clean all by themselves.

_____ 5. Mr. Williams never has help with the class.

Inference

_____ 1. The principal likes Mr. Williams.

_____ 2. The children learn a lot.

_____ 3. Mr. Williams never uses books.

_____ 4. The children are bored.

_____ 5. The children are afraid of Mr. Williams.

Name _____ *Date* _____

Write two details to support each main idea.

Paragraph One: Mr. Williams uses many ways of teaching.

_____ .

_____ .

Paragraph Two: The children work very hard.

_____ .

_____ .

Paragraph Three: The parents like Mr. Williams.

_____ .

_____ .

STRUCTURES

I	wish	that	I	were	rich.	(Present situation)
I	wish	that	I	had left	earlier.	(Past situation)
I	wish	that	he	would help	us.	(Future situation)

VOCABULARY

Nouns	Verbs	Adjectives	Other
amusement	invite	extra	_____
community	_____	frightened	_____
frog	_____	_____	_____
mouse (mice)	_____	_____	_____
plant	_____	_____	_____
principal	_____	_____	_____
roller coaster	_____	_____	_____
umbrella	_____	_____	_____
_____	_____	_____	_____
_____	_____	_____	_____

HOMEWORK

A. Review the **Practice Wishing** section and be ready to answer the questions during the next class.

B. Write answers to the **More Wishes** section on a separate sheet of paper.

C. Prepare two sentences about yourself using each of the *wish* patterns. Be ready to say all six sentences during the next class. Try to tell the truth.

D. Look at Picture 13 on page 104. Write five *wish* sentences about the man in the picture.

1. _____.

2. _____.

3. _____.

Name _____ *Date* _____

4. _____.

5. _____.

LISTENING EXERCISE

Fill in the missing words.

1. I wish that I _____ rich.

2. Wanda wishes that she _____ the key.

3. We wish that we _____ it.

4. They wish that the class _____.

5. Dan wishes that the store _____ open.

6. I wish that I _____ tennis.

7. The parents wish that he _____ in town.

8. Ruth wished that she _____ more.

9. We wish that the weather _____ warmer.

10. They wish that they _____ him.

Unit 13

PICTURE TO TALK ABOUT

People all over the world know the Statue of Liberty as a symbol of the United States. The teacher will read a short history of the statue. Repeat each sentence. Then say the sentences to another student. Later write in the missing words.

Pan American World Airways, Inc.

PICTURE 19

Name _____ Date _____

1. The Statue of Liberty _____ _____ by Auguste Bartholdi.

2. It _____ _____ to the United States by France.

3. The statue _____ _____ of copper.

4. It _____ _____ in Paris in 1884.

5. Then it _____ _____ to the United States.

6. It _____ _____ on Bedloe's Island in New York Harbor.

7. That name _____ _____ to Liberty Island in 1960.

8. The Statue of Liberty _____ _____ by thousands of people every month.

PASSIVES

The sentences above contain passive verbs. In most sentences the subject performs the action. But in passive sentences the subject receives the action.

Active: Aguste Bartholdi designed the Statue of Liberty.

Passive: The Statue of Liberty was designed by Aguste Bartholdi.

Use the passive in the following situations:

Situation 1:   when the receiver of the action is more important than the performer of the action

The Statue of Liberty was designed by Aguste Bartholdi.

(The statue is more famous than the man.)

Situation 2:   when the people who performed the action are unimportant or unknown

The statue was placed on Bedloe's Island.

(We don't know the names of the people who did it.)

Situation 3:   when you are discussing history

The statue was given to the United States by France.

(It was an historical event.)

Passive sentences always contain some tense of the verb *to be* plus a Past Participle.

	To Be +	Past Participle	
The statue	*is*	*made*	of copper.
It	*was*	*placed*	on Bedloe's Island.

PRACTICE PASSIVES

Work in pairs. Take turns changing the following active sentences into passive sentences. In these sentences you don't know who performed the actions.

Example: 1. Someone broke the window last night.

The window *was broken* last night.

2. They changed Bill's telephone number.

3. Someone found my wallet this morning.

4. They grew these oranges in Florida.

5. Someone left the children alone.

6. They moved my car.

7. Someone opened the window.

8. Someone rented the apartment before I arrived.

MORE PASSIVE PRACTICE

Work in pairs again. Sometimes passive sentences end in *by* + Noun. This shows who or what performed the action. Take turns changing the following sentences from active to passive. Add *by* + Noun at the end of each one.

Example: 1. Three men carried the sofa.

The sofa *was carried* by three men.

2. A cigarette caused the fire.

3. A dog bit the baby.

4. The teacher checked my test.

5. An old lady drove the car.

6. A rich family gave the party.

7. A thousand people saw the movie.

8. A sixteen-year-old girl wrote the book.

PAST TENSE VS. PRESENT TENSE

Work in groups of four or five. Take turns changing the following sentences from active to passive. If the active sentence has a present tense verb, use the present tense of *to be* + Past Participle in the passive. If the active sentence has a past tense verb, use the past tense of *to be* + Past Participle, and so forth.

Examples: 1. They are speaking French.

French *is being spoken*.

2. Someone closed the windows.

The windows *were closed*.

3. Someone is helping Ruth.

4. Someone explained the answer.

Name _____ Date _____

5. You make a cake with eggs.

6. They are finishing the work.

7. They invited you.

8. Someone sang a beautiful song.

9. They are painting my apartment.

10. They close the store every Sunday.

WRITING PRACTICE

Write five sentences from the **More Passive Practice** section.

1. _____.

2. _____.

3. _____.

4. _____.

5. _____.

READING PASSAGE

Every month thousands of tourists visit New York City. Their reasons for choosing New York are many. Some come to see historical places like the Statue of Liberty. Others are attracted by the night clubs and theaters. Many enjoy shopping in the world's largest stores. And some come to New York just because it's big.

People from other parts of the United States move to New York by the thousands each year. Some come to get better jobs. Others want to attend one of New York's fine universities. Dancers, actors, and painters are attracted by the city's rich cultural life. Still others are bored with small-town life and want the excitement of the big city.

Careful planning is needed to make your stay in New York City a success. Be sure that you don't arrive during the rush hour. Weekdays from 7:30 to 9:00 A.M. and 4:30 to 6:00 P.M. travel on the streets is slow and difficult. Choose a hotel that is near the center of the city. And be sure to bring plenty of money. It's no fun to see hundreds of exciting things to do and not have the money to do them.

READING QUESTIONS

Finding Details

Write two details to support each main idea.

Paragraph One: Tourists visit New York City for many reasons.

_____.

_____.

Paragraph Two: People from other parts of the United States move to New York for many reasons.

_____.

_____.

Paragraph Three: Careful planning is necessary for an enjoyable visit.

_____.

_____.

VOCABULARY PRACTICE

Fill in the blanks using the following eight words:

actors	attracts	history	rush hour
attend	designed	place	world

1. The _____ is a very big place.

2. Have you studied the _____ of your country?

3. Beautiful dresses are _____ in Paris.

4. Students _____ universities.

5. Don't try to drive during the _____.

6. The city _____ dancers and painters.

7. _____ the glass on the table carefully.

8. _____ work in theaters.

STRUCTURES

Ruth	is being	helped.	
A cake	is	made	with eggs.
You	were	invited.	

VOCABULARY

Nouns	*Verbs*	*Adjectives*	*Other*
actor	attend	cultural	_____
copper	attract	_____	_____
history	bite – bit – bitten	_____	_____
orange	design	_____	_____
rush hour	place	_____	_____
symbol	_____	_____	_____
university	_____	_____	_____
world	_____	_____	_____
_____	_____	_____	_____
_____	_____	_____	_____

HOMEWORK

A. Memorize five of the sentences under Picture 19. Be ready to say them out loud during the next class.

B. Review the **Practice Passive** section. Write five of the answers on a separate sheet of paper.

C. Make up a passive sentence using each of these past participles:

broken   cooked   driven   helped   played

opened   washed

D. Change the following sentences from active to passive.

1. Someone is selling that car.

_____.

2. The city is spending a lot of money.

_____.

3. They play baseball on Saturdays.

_____.

4. The fire burned two houses.

_____.

5. Someone locked the door.

_____.

LISTENING EXERCISE

Fill in the missing words.

1. The window _____ _____.

2. That work _____ _____ right now.

3. They _____ _____ by 9:00.

4. The party _____ _____ by Dan.

5. The clothes _____ _____.

6. The song _____ _____ slowly.

7. Many parks _____ _____ in New York City.

8. That machine _____ _____ by Mr. Wilson.

9. Dinner _____ _____ right now.

10. The tourists _____ _____ by bus.

Unit 14

PICTURE TO TALK ABOUT

Paula Cavero wants a career, not a husband and family. The teacher will describe her life using ten idioms. Be sure that you understand each sentence. Then repeat each one. After that say the sentences to another student. Later write in the missing words.

A. T. & T. Photo Center

PICTURE 20

Name _____ Date _____

1. Paula doesn't want to _____ children.

2. She isn't _____ office work or teaching either. She has always wanted to be a telephone installer.

3. She _____ when she was sixteen.

4. Her parents wanted her to _____, but she didn't. She took a six-month training program at the phone company.

5. Paula _____ quickly. She's one of their best workers now.

6. They _____ her to do a good job.

7. They _____ her.

8. Paula has to _____ noisy dogs.

9. Sometimes talkative children _____.

10. But _____ she likes her job.

IDIOMS

An idiom is a group of words that has a meaning different from the meaning of each separate word. For example "*put up with* noisy dogs" in sentence 8 does not mean that Paula puts a noisy dog above her head with something else. *Put up with* means "accept."

Copy the correct meaning from Column B after the idiom in Column A.

Name _____ Date _____

Column A		Column B
bring up _____		decide
catch on _____		make you nervous
can't do without _____		think differently
*change your mind _____		help to grow
count on _____		most of the time
cut out for _____		accept
*get on your nerves _____		must have; need
*make up your mind _____		good at a certain type of work
on the whole _____		believe someone will do a good job
put up with _____		learn

PARAPHRASE PRACTICE

Work in pairs. Take turns paraphrasing the sentences below using the ten idioms.

Example: 1. I hope that you will think differently soon.

I hope that you will *change your mind* soon.

2. I'm not good with children.

I'm not _____ teaching.

3. I hate hot weather, but I accept it.

I _____ hot weather.

*Your, my, his, her, our, their.

4. Mrs. Brown is taking care of four children.

Mrs. Brown _____ four children.

5. Loud music makes me nervous.

Loud music _____.

6. I'm happy in most ways.

_____ I'm happy.

7. I learn fast.

I _____ fast.

8. You have to decide before tomorrow night.

You have to _____ before tomorrow
night.

9. Fish need water.

Fish _____ water.

10. I'm sure that you will do a good job.

I'm sure that I can _____you.

FILL-IN-PRACTICE

Work in pairs. Take turns filling in the missing idioms.

Example: 1. A baby _____ its mother.

2. I don't like to fight. I'm not _____ fighting.

3. I think that you are wrong. I hope that you _____.

4. The crying of the baby _____.

5. My mother _____ four children.

6. Which shirt will you buy? You have to _____.

7. I'm a good worker. You can _____ me.

8. That lesson was difficult. I didn't _____.

9. _____ I like living here.

10. If you live in a big city, you have to _____ the dirt.

QUESTIONS AND ANSWERS

Work in groups of four or five. Take turns asking and answering the questions below using the ten idioms.

Example: 1. Do you like coffee?

Yes, I do. I *can't do without* coffee.

2. Is math easy for you to learn?

3. Have you decided yet?

4. Does Dan always do a good job?

5. How do you feel about cold weather?

6. Do you enjoy hard work?

7. Will you think differently next week?

8. How many children does Mrs. Cavero have?

9. Does Paula like being a telephone installer?

10. What makes Paula nervous?

Name _____ *Date* _____

WRITING PRACTICE

Review the **Questions and Answers** above. Then write five answers in the blanks below.

1. _____ .

2. _____ .

3. _____ .

4. _____ .

5. _____ .

READING PASSAGE

In the past certain kinds of jobs were closed to women. But recently women have been taking many new kinds of jobs. You can see women working in gas stations. The telephone company has hired many female telephone installers. Women are beginning to get important jobs as bank managers and corporation presidents. More and more women are going into law and medicine.

One reason women are doing more kinds of jobs is that the laws have changed. In the past, if a man and a woman applied for the same job, the man would get it. Now the employer must hire the person who can do the job best. Another law says that some businesses must hire fifty percent women. Still another law says that some employers can't write a newspaper advertisement asking for a *man* or a *woman*. They must advertise for a *person* to do the job.

Some men are now doing jobs which used to be called "women's work." There are more male nurses and male secretaries than ever before. Men are becoming elementary school teachers. Some are even becoming homemakers. This sometimes happens when the couple finds out that the wife can earn more than the husband. What a surprise for the man who learns that he can be good at a "woman's job"—and enjoy it!

Name _____ *Date* _____

Main Idea

Reread each paragraph and state its main idea in one sentence.

Paragraph One: _____.

Paragraph Two: _____.

Paragraph Three: _____.

VOCABULARY PRACTICE

Fill in the blanks using the following eight words:

advertise	career	couple	kind
apply	corporation	hire	quickly

1. That company is going to _____ six new workers.

2. I want a _____ in banking.

3. What _____ of job do you want?

4. That _____ has three children.

5. Answer the questions _____.

6. I'm going to _____ for a job as a secretary.

7. They never _____ in the newspaper.

8. American Motors is a very large _____.

STRUCTURES

See the ten idioms introduced on page 162.

*Name*_____ *Date* _____

VOCABULARY

Nouns	Verbs	Adjectives	Other
career	advertise	_____	quickly
corporation	apply	_____	recently
couple	fight	_____	_____
fish	hire	_____	_____
homemaker	_____	_____	_____
installer	_____	_____	_____
kind	_____	_____	_____
president	_____	_____	_____
training	_____	_____	_____
_____	_____	_____	_____
_____	_____	_____	_____

HOMEWORK

A. Memorize the ten sentences on page 161. Be ready to say them out loud during the next class.

B. Paraphrase the following sentences using the ten idioms. Write them on a separate sheet of paper.

1. Please decide quickly.

2. I understood quickly.

3. I need your help.

4. Tests make me nervous.

5. I am usually happy with your work.

Name_____ Date _____

C. Be ready to answer these questions using the idioms.

    1. How many children do you have?

    2. Do you like taxes?

    3. Does a fat person like running?

    4. Do you think he can help us?

    5. Do you feel differently about it today?

D. Make up five original sentences using the idioms. Write them below.

    1. _____.

    2. _____.

    3. _____.

    4. _____.

    5. _____.

LISTENING EXERCISE

Fill in the missing words.

    1. I have to _____ that noise.

    2. They _____ two children.

    3. _____ she's a hard worker.

    4. Please _____.

    5. He _____.

    6. I _____ my medicine.

Name _____ Date _____

7. You _____ fast.

8. You can _____ me.

9. I can't _____.

10. He's not _____ office work.

Unit 15

PICTURE TO TALK ABOUT

This is Batavia, New York. The Sylvania Company in Batavia wants to hire Bill Long. The job is interesting and the money is good. But if he takes the job, Bill will have to leave New York City. The teacher will describe Bill's thoughts. Repeat each sentence. Then say the sentences to another student. Later write in the missing words.

The Daily News, Batavia, New York

PICTURE 21

Name _____ *Date* _____

1. Bill doesn't know _____ he wants to live in a small town.

2. He's not sure _____ Batavia is a nice place to live.

3. _____ it's small, Batavia has a lot of corporations.

4. _____ he doesn't know anyone there, he's sure the people are friendly.

5. Bill can't decide _____ to say *yes* or *no* to Sylvania.

6. He doesn't know _____ to go, or to stay in New York.

7. _____ he visits Batavia, he'll never make up his mind.

8. _____ he decides soon, Sylvania will find someone else.

ALTHOUGH, UNLESS, **AND** *WHETHER*

Sentences 3 and 4 use *although* clauses to describe a situation, followed by a main clause that describes a surprising result.

Although Clause (Situation)	*Main* Clause (Surprising Result)
Although it's small,	Batavia has a lot of corporations.

Now look at a *because* clause that is always followed by a normal result.

Because Clause (Situation)	*Main* Clause (Normal Result)
Because it's small,	Batavia has few corporations.

Sentences 7 and 8 use *unless* clauses. *Unless* is the same as *if +
not.*

Unless Clause	*Main* Clause (Result)
Unless he visits Batavia,	he'll never make up his mind.
If he *doesn't* visit Batavia,	he'll never make up his mind.

Name _____ *Date* ___ _____

Sentences 1 and 2 use *whether* or *not*. It means the same as *if*.

Whether or Not

Bill doesn't know *whether or not* he wants to live in a small town.

Bill doesn't know   *if*   he wants to live in a small town.

Sentences 5 and 6 use *whether* + *infinitive*. Here the *whether* means "if he wants."

Whether +   Infinitive

He can't decide *whether*   *to say* yes or no to Sylvania.

He can't decide *if he wants*   *to say* yes or no to Sylvania.

ALTHOUGH **AND** *UNLESS*

Work in pairs. Take turns making sentences with *although* and *unless* clauses by combining an item from Column A with one from Column B.

Example: 1. Although I washed the floor, it was still dirty.

Column A	Column B
1. Although I washed the floor,	A. I couldn't remember his name.
2. Unless you take this medicine	B. he will be hungry soon.
3. Although he's very old,	C. it was still dirty.
4. Unless he is tired	D. he sang very well.
5. Although I had met him,	E. he gets up early.
6. Unless I feed the dog,	F. my father can run fast.
7. Unless you tell me the answer	G. you won't feel better.
8. Although he was nervous	H. I will be angry.

Name _____ Date _____

WHETHER AND WHETHER OR NOT

Work in groups of three. One person asks the question. The second person answers using a sentence with a *whether or not* clause. The third person paraphrases the answer using *whether + Infinitive.*

Example: 1. Will you study French?

I don't know whether or not I'll study French.

I don't know whether to study French or Spanish.

2. Will you go home?

3. Will you wear your red coat?

4. Will you leave in the morning?

5. Will you play baseball?

6. Will you go by train?

PARAPHRASE PRACTICE

Work in groups of four or five. Take turns paraphrasing the following sentences using *although, unless, whether or not,* and *whether + Infinitive.*

Example: 1. If I don't leave now, I'll be late.

Unless I leave now, I'll be late.

2. It was warm, but I wore a coat.

3. I can't decide if I should buy a big car.

4. He doesn't know if he should hire Dan.

5. If she doesn't study, she'll fail the test.

6. He is rich, but he never spends any money.

7. He's not sure if he should drive north.

Name _____ Date _____

8. If they don't win, they'll be sad.

9. She was late, but the boss didn't notice.

10. They can't decide if they should visit Florida.

WRITING PRACTICE

Write the answers to five of the **Paraphrase Practice** items.

1. _____.

2. _____.

3. _____.

4. _____.

5. _____.

READING PASSAGE

The reading passage in Unit 14 tells about Americans who are moving to big cities. At the same time, many Americans are leaving the cities and looking for the "good life" in the country. Although they think they know what they want, they don't always find it.

Unless you know something about small-town life, you may be in for some big surprises. There are not so many job opportunities there. People are not always happy about having newcomers move in. They like to keep things the way they are. And although there is usually a movie theater and a couple of restaurants, there isn't a lot to do at night.

But if you're looking for a more relaxed way of life, if you want to save money, and if you can make your own good times, small-town life may be for you. Before you decide whether or not to leave the city, spend a couple weeks in a village. Look around and talk to people. Think what it would be like to live there fifty-two weeks a year. And then, if you're sure, you can make the big move.

READING QUESTIONS

Write T in front of true sentences and F in front of false ones.

Fact

_____ 1. Many people are moving to small towns.

_____ 2. Some people don't find the "good life" in small towns.

_____ 3. There are few job opportunities in small towns.

_____ 4. There is a lot to do at night in small towns.

_____ 5. Small-town people like to keep things like they were in the past.

Inference

_____ 1. Small-town people can be unfriendly to newcomers.

_____ 2. Some city people don't really know what they want.

_____ 3. The surprises you find in a small town are always nice.

_____ 4. Life is slower in small towns.

_____ 5. It's a good idea to move to a small town before you visit it.

VOCABULARY PRACTICE

Fill in the blanks using the following eight words:

apply	hired	newcomer	opportunities
couple	look around	normal	village

1. I just came here. I'm a _____.

2. That _____ has two children.

3. Bill was _____ by Sylvania.

4. A very small city is called a _____.

5. There are many _____ to work in a big city.

6. Did you _____ for a job with Sylvania?

7. The temperature feels _____ today.

8. Go to the library and _____.

STRUCTURES

Although he is rich,	he never spends money.	
Unless you are rich,	you can't spend a lot of money.	
He's not sure	*whether or not*	he should leave right now.
He's not sure	*whether to leave*	in the morning or the evening.

VOCABULARY

Nouns	*Verbs*	*Adjectives*	*Other*
newcomer	look around	normal	_____
opportunity	_____	_____	_____
village	_____	_____	_____
_____	_____	_____	_____
_____	_____	_____	_____
_____	_____		

HOMEWORK

A. Review the **Although** and **Unless** section. Think of original completions for the Column A items. Be ready to say your completions during the next class.

B. Be ready to make sentences using *whether + Infinitive* and *whether or not* from the following items:

   1. have breakfast

   2. take a plane

   3. sit down

   4. stay home

   5. call Ruth

C. Think of completions from the following sentences. Be ready to say at least one completion for each sentence during the next class.

   1. Although it was cold, _____.

   2. Unless you are careful, _____.

   3. They aren't sure whether or not _____.

   4. He can't decide whether to _____.

D. Write two original sentences using each of the following:

   Although: 1. _____.

                2. _____.

   Unless: 1. _____.

                2. _____.

Name _____ Date _____

Whether or not	1. _____.
	2. _____.
Whether + Infinitive	1. _____.
	2. _____.

LISTENING EXERCISE

Fill in the missing words.

1. _____ it's small, I love it.

2. He can't decide _____ to go.

3. He'll be there _____ he's busy.

4. I can't go _____ I want to.

5. Ruth isn't sure _____ to buy the Ford.

6. _____ you stay home, you won't see it.

7. I can't decide _____ to buy it.

8. _____ I'm tired, I'll do my homework.

9. He's not sure _____ to keep it or give it away.

10. She'll do it _____ she forgets.

Review

REVIEW QUESTIONS FOR UNIT 1-5

Write a, b, or c in front of the number to show which word or words complete the sentence correctly.

_____ 1. Please [(a) listen me to   (b) listen her   (c) listen to her].

_____ 2. They [(a) bring back them   (b) bring them back
(c) bring back] on Tuesdays.

_____ 3. I studied [(a) after that   (b) until   (c) afterward] 2:00.

_____ 4. I had lunch. [(a) After   (b) Afterward   (c) Until] I
played tennis.

_____ 5. It's good [(a) see   (b) to see   (c) saw] you.

_____ 6. How far [(a) it is   (b) does it   (c) is it] to Alaska?

_____ 7. They [(a) have sitting   (b) been sitting   (c) have been
sitting] there for an hour.

_____ 8. Where [(a) have you been   (b) you have been   (c) you've
been] living?

_____ 9. They [(a) had   (b) asked   (c) got] me wear a warm coat.

_Name_____ _Date_ _____

_____ 10. They didn't make him [(a) going (b) to go (c) go].

_____ 11. You don't smoke, [(a) are you (b) do you (c) don't you]?

_____ 12. He has left already, [(a) has he (b) hasn't he (c) did he]?

_____ 13. Los Angeles is [(a) in (b) on (c) at] California.

_____ 14. He lives [(a) in (b) on (c) at] Main Street.

_____ 15. I met her [(a) in (b) on (c) at] winter.

_____ 16. We arrived [(a) in (b) on (c) at] 8:15.

_____ 17. [(a) Everyone (b) Anyone (c) One] is watching television.

_____ 18. I don't want [(a) nothing (b) something (c) anything].

_____ 19. I'm not going [(a) nowhere (b) somewhere (c) anywhere].

_____ 20. Did you see [(a) no one (b) something (c) anywhere]?

REVIEW QUESTIONS FOR UNITS 6-10

_____ 1. [(a) Each (b) Every (c) All] the people are working hard.

_____ 2. I see him [(a) every (b) all (c) all the] day.

_____ 3. [(a) Either (b) Neither (c) Or] John or Jim will be there.

_____ 4. Both Ruth [(a) or (b) nor (c) and] Don will attend.

_____ 5. We [(a) were (b) have been (c) had been] home for ten minutes when the phone rang.

Name _____ Date _____

_____ 6. I had stood for an hour when I finally [(a) find   (b) found (c) had found] a seat.

_____ 7. He said that he [(a) learns   (b) learning   (c) had learned] to speak French.

_____ 8. She said that she [(a) was   (b) will be   (c) were] happy that you had gone to the party.

_____ 9. It was [(a) such big chair   (b) such big chairs   (c) so big] that I couldn't move it.

_____ 10. It was [(a) so heavy   (b) such a heavy   (c) such heavy] table that I couldn't pick it up.

_____ 11. The green one is pretty [(a) and is too   (b) and so is (c) and neither is] the red one.

_____ 12. Florida is not cold [(a) and neither is   (b) and so is (c) and also] California.

_____ 13. If you had arrived earlier, you (a) would see   (b) will see (c) would have seen] her.

_____ 14. If Bill had asked them, they [(a) would help   (b) will help (c) would have helped] him.

_____ 15. There are [(a) 12   (b) 16   (c) 3] ounces in one pound.

_____ 16. A meter is almost the same as [(a) an inch   (b) a yard (c) a foot].

_____ 17. I like to work [(a) by myself   (b) to myself   (c) of myself].

_____ 18. They completed it [(a) theirselves   (b) themselves (c) themself].

_____ 19. That movie was [(a) interest   (b) interested (c) interesting].

_____ 20. Is he an [(a) interest   (b) interesting   (c) amused] man?

Name _____ _Date_ _____

_____ 1. I enjoy [(a) to drive   (b) drive   (c) driving].

_____ 2. They suggested [(a) to stop   (b) stopping   (c) stop] for a few minutes.

_____ 3. Did you practice [(a) how to drive   (b) to drive (c) driving] before you took the test?

_____ 4. I enjoyed [(a) swam   (b) to swim   (c) swimming].

_____ 5. Bill wishes that [(a) he stays   (b) he will stay   (c) he had stayed] home today.

_____ 6. We wish that [(a) it will   (b) it were   (c) it would] stop.

_____ 7. If I [(a) am   (b) was   (c) were] older, I would buy a car.

_____ 8. I wish that the weather [(a) would   (b) were   (c) will be] nice.

_____ 9. My seat [(a) is change   (b) was change   (c) was changed].

_____ 10. The door [(a) was opened   (b) were opened   (c) opened] by two tall men.

_____ 11. In Paris, French [(a) speaks   (b) is speaking   (c) is spoken].

_____ 12. A beautiful song [(a) is singing   (b) is being sung   (c) was being sang].

_____ 13. I can't [(a) put up with   (b) catch on   (c) bring up] hot weather.

_____ 14. Please decide! You must [(a) count on   (b) make up your mind   (c) do without].

_____ 15. Can you [(a) on the whole   (b) count on   (c) catch on] him?

Name _____ _Date_ _____

_____ 16. I need you. I can't [(a) do without   (b) put up with
(c) cut out for] you.

_____ 17. [(a) Although   (b) Unless   (c) Whether] he was busy,
he helped us out.

_____ 18. [(a) Although   (b) Unless   (c) Whether] it rains, we will
have the picnic tomorrow.

_____ 19. I'll have to decide [(a) if   (b) unless   (c) whether or not]
to attend.

_____ 20. He can't decide (a) unless   (b) whether or not
(c) although] he should buy the car.

CLOZE TEST

Read the passage below. Twenty words are missing. In each blank
write one word that will complete the sentence correctly. _Do not_ write
more than one word.

Ruth and Dan recently moved from the city to the country. Dan
got a job in a factory and Ruth works in a restaurant.

At first they couldn't decide (1. _____) or not to

leave (2. _____) city. They had a (3. _____)

of friends. Ruth and Dan (4. _____) been living in the

(5. _____) for a long time. (6. _____) they

were sad to (7. _____) their friends, they decided

(8. _____) go.

They are enjoying (9. _____) new life. Dan suggested

(10. _____) a boat. So now (11. _____)

spend their weekends at (12. _____) small lake near

their (13. _____). Life is more relaxing

(14. _____) the country than it (15. _____)

Name _____ Date _____

been in the city. Dan (16. _____) beginning to get fat.

(17. _____) he starts eating less, (18. _____)

will have a problem.

(19. _____) talk about returning to

(20. _____) city, but they won't. They love their new

life too much.

Fill-ins

The following fill-ins are used in the introductory sections of each lesson. (When a lesson covers two different grammar points, there are two introductory sections.) If a student is using the book without a teacher, he or she will need this material to get started on each section of the lesson.

Fill-ins for the remaining parts of each lesson are given in the answer keys found in the Teacher's Manual.

FILL-INS

Unit 1, page 2

listened to, looked at, laughed at, talked about, looked for, Fill out, Pick out, Check out, Bring back, call up

page 6

before, until, after, Afterwards, After that, Afterwards, after, before, until, After that

Unit 2, page 19

bought, have been living, have been working, are sitting, have been talking, has been smoking, invited, has been wanting, called, have been waiting

Name _____ Date _____

Unit 3, page 28

got his father to take, had Danny wear, didn't make Danny go, got him to go, had Danny practice, made him go

page 32

don't you, do you, won't it, will you, didn't you, did you

Unit 4, page 41

in, in, in, in, on, at and in, in, in, on, at

page 44

in, in, in, on, on, at and in, in, in, on, on, at

Unit 5, page 52

Everyone, No one, anyone, Someone, Everything, anything, Nothing, something, everywhere, nowhere, anywhere, somewhere

page 57

The first two, The next two, The last three, a big new, a little old, a tall young, a blue cotton, blue denim, black leather, a green plastic

Unit 6, page 65

All the men, Each man, each other, Not all, All workers, Every employee

page 69

Both . . . and, Neither . . . nor, Either . . . or, Both . . . and, Neither . . . nor, Either . . . or

Unit 7, page 78

had lived, had broken, had covered, had repaired, hadn't moved, had built

page 81

was, was, was planning, was coming, wanted, needed

Name _____ Date _____

page 83

had thought, had been, had thought, had been, had started, had cleaned

Unit 8, page 92

such a good team, such good luck, such a good player, such a big salary, such long legs, such bright sunshine, such long trips

page 95

and so is, and neither is, and so did, and neither did, and so has, and neither has

Unit 9, page 105

hadn't left, might have finished, hadn't started, could have gotten, had had, could have rented, would have asked, hadn't been, would have helped, had asked, would have died, hadn't taken

page 110

16, 1,000, 28, 450, 12, 3, 100, 2.5, 30, 90

Unit 10, page 119

by himself, himself, to himself, by himself, himself, of himself

page 122

excited, surprised, interested, tired, bored, exciting, surprising, interesting, tiring, boring

page 124

people, things

Unit 11, page 133

driving, buying, driving, having, getting, eating, driving, driving, having, finding

Name _____ _Date_ _____

Unit 12, page 143

were, was going, felt, had stayed, hadn't brought, hadn't gotten,
would stop, would make, would relax

Unit 13, page 151

was designed, was given, is made, was finished, was sent, was placed,
was changed, is visited

Unit 14, page 160

bring up, cut out for, made up her mind, change her mind, caught on,
count on, can't do without, put up with, get on her nerves, on the whole

Unit 15, page 170

whether or not, whether or not, Although, Although, whether,
whether, Unless, Unless

Name _____ Date _____